AF259223

World Champion, Olympic Medalist & MBA

NOELLE PIKUS PACE

NO EXCUSES.

HOW 60 SECONDS OF OWNERSHIP CAN TRANSFORM YOUR LIFE, YOUR TEAM AND YOUR RESULTS

NO EXCUSES: How 60 Seconds of Ownership Can Transform Your Life, Your Team, and Your Results

ISBN: 978-1-7331370-2-7
Printed in the United States of America
First Edition

For bulk orders, speaking engagements, or corporate training inquiries, visit:
www.noellepikuspace.com

DEDICATION

To my family, Janson, Lacee, Traycen, Payton, and Makai, for always making me laugh, even on the toughest days. We did it! And we'll continue to write our beautiful story together.

To my parents, for letting me park my 1999 Leprechaun motorhome on the side of your house so I could actually write this. You've always made space for my dreams.

To the readers who skipped straight to this page. Bold move. I respect it. You took action. And action removes excuses.

And finally, to caffeine. You know what you did.

MY PROMISE

I believe that real transformation begins with simplicity.

When you stop overcomplicating things, you open the door to the life, the leadership, and the results you actually want.

So, here's my promise to you.

60 seconds of courage will lead you to the life you want.

If you read this book and use these tools, you'll stop waiting for the right moment and start living your life like it matters.

You'll learn how to shut down excuses the second they show up.

You'll make clearer decisions. You'll move faster. You'll act even when fear tells you not to. And when you do, your habits strengthen. Your results become consistent. And your purpose gets louder than the pressure.

And let's be honest.
NO EXCUSES without mercy would be impossible.

That's why this book puts "Mercy in the Middle" at the center of the chapters. It belongs right in the middle of every choice you make.

With mercy, **NO EXCUSES** becomes the most honest, human, and compassionate way to live.

Use these tools, and the shift in your life won't stay small. Your confidence will grow. Your direction will sharpen. And you'll live each day with intention. You'll feel it in how you lead yourself, how you love your people, and how you show up for your team.

The toughest person you will ever lead is yourself.

These 60 seconds tools will change your day. Repeat them and they'll change your life.

INTRODUCTION

THE ACCIDENT

October 19, 2005.

I never saw the bobsled coming.

One moment I was sitting beside the track in Calgary, Canada, talking with my teammates. And the next I was on the asphalt, 30 feet away, unable to move.

A 1,400-pound 4-man bobsled flew out of the track and hit me head-on. And my leg shattered so badly that my heel touched my calf.

I tried to stand but I immediately collapsed.

My teammate, Lea Ann, ran to my side. She was a nurse and a firefighter by trade and she knew what this kind of injury meant. So, she gently pressed my head back to the ground, wrapped her arms around me, and whispered that everything was going to be okay.

Then, right there on the road, she offered a prayer out loud to God that I would be all right.

The medics arrived quickly.

Lea Ann leaned over me and said,

"All right, Noelle, this is really going to hurt. They have to set your leg. Your bones are out. To get you to the hospital, they have to put them back into place."

Then I heard the medic say, *"We're going to do it on the count of 3. Ready? 1... 2..."* They didn't make it to 3.

On 2, pain tore through my body so violently I couldn't breathe. I only remember fragments.

A crowd gathered.
The sound of the stretcher.
Hands moving.

As they lifted me into the ambulance and the doors closed, every bump and turn sent shockwaves through my body.

Then the pain took over.

I woke up in a hospital room while a nurse explained what would happen next. A titanium rod. Multiple screws. Infection prevention. I managed to say 3 words before the anesthesia pulled me under.

"Call my husband."

When I woke up after surgery, I didn't recognize my leg. It was swollen, stapled, and carved with incisions. After 13 failed attempts to start an IV, the trauma unit was called in.

My body felt like a pincushion.

The hospital was full that day and the staff told me that the only space available for recovery was in the waiting room. Beside the check-in desk, and the vending machines.

My IV dripped next to a rack of Frito-Lay chips.

In just a few hours, I'd gone from world-class athlete to "aisle three, salty snacks."

When I turned my head, I saw a mother and daughter leaning against each other, waiting for news of a loved one. At one point, a nurse told me she couldn't leave my side until I used the bedpan.

So, there I was.
In a hospital waiting room.
Surrounded by strangers.
Humiliated.
Broken.

Earlier that day, I was ranked first in the world in the sport of skeleton and hopeful for my future. By nightfall, that future was gone.

When my husband, Janson, arrived, he stayed beside me. Advocating. Asking questions. Fighting for better care.

At one point my oxygen levels plummeted. Critically low. My heart rate slowed, and I drifted out of consciousness.

Janson yelled down the hall for help. A nurse came in and began hitting the machine. Insisting that it must be broken. Minutes later, the trauma unit rushed in again. My oxygen levels rose and I stabilized.

I remember thinking, *I'm still alive.*

It was one of the hardest nights of my life.

MY RECOVERY

Recovery wasn't a comeback. It was a calendar.

Physical therapy appointments. More surgeries. Pain medication. Check-ups.

The doctors weren't sure if I'd ever walk normally again. Let alone race down an icy track at 90 miles an hour.

When you're stripped of what defines you, you clearly see what's underneath the surface.

I saw fear. Frustration. And dozens of excuses lining up in my mind like second graders in a school lunch line.

They showed up all at once.

You've already done enough.

You have every reason to quit.

No one would blame you.

And honestly, they sounded reasonable.

Excuses always do.

I tried to stay positive. But depression crept in. I expected to pick up where I left off. To be number one again. But instead, when I returned to compete, I finished at the bottom of the field.

My injury broke more than my leg. It fractured me mentally and emotionally. And the gap between where I was and where I wanted to be felt impossible to reach.

I missed out on the Olympic Games and I was ashamed that I couldn't live up to the expectations that had once defined me. And when that season finally ended, I felt empty.

I remember curling up on our cold kitchen floor. Sobbing until the tears wouldn't come and my head felt like it would split open.

Quitting seemed like the only option. And it wasn't the last time that thought would show up. Because one thing consistently gets in the way of progress.

Excuses.

HOW I LEARNED ABOUT EXCUSES

I'm a pretty resilient person. I tend to see the positive in most situations. But in my life, my research, interactions with others, and the stories in this book, the pattern is clear.

When excuses take over, energy drains and progress slows.

When action replaces an excuse, energy increases. Anxiety drops. And results improve.

Every. Single. Time.

Life is full of ups and downs. It's a series of moments where you choose again and again. And rock bottom has a way of forcing a choice.

After my injury, I learned that I had 2 choices.
I could stay where I was. Or I could start again.

I chose to start again.

I made it back to compete on the World Cup circuit for the U.S. team. And every day brought the same decision.

Make an excuse. Or make progress.

I rebuilt my leg. And my belief. One choice at a time. And one year later, I became the World Champion.

I definitely didn't do it alone, and I'm still learning.

That race wasn't about beating anyone else. It was about proving to myself that excuses didn't define or limit me. It was a reminder that progress is possible when you stop letting doubt, blame, and justifications steer your life.

Every medal, every mile, and every moment after that has been built on that same truth.

You always have a choice.

I learned this again years later, in a very different way.

My brother Rob died unexpectedly in an accident in 2023. The year he passed, he ran with the bulls in Spain, bought homes for refugees in Ukraine, and helped people who were struggling to find their footing.

He lived a **NO EXCUSES** life.

And like funerals often do, his death forced me to look hard at my own life.

I saw places where I had drifted. Where I had played small. Where I had hidden behind comfort and fear. I realized that somewhere along the way, I had moved away from the life I actually wanted to live.

Here's the truth.

Every heartbreak, setback, and season of life comes down to the same choice.

Step forward.
Or stay stuck.
All it takes is one decision.

So, the week after Rob's funeral, I made a decision before I could talk myself out of it. I surprised Janson with a 1999 Class-C motor home. We had talked about camping with our kids for years and always found reasons to wait.

That week, we didn't wait.
We went.
And it changed everything.

NO EXCUSES began creating momentum in my family, my leadership, and my life again.

Mountain biking. New friends. Backyard movies. Hard conversations. Forgiveness. Finished projects. Relief. Fulfillment. Growth.

Over the years, challenges have come to me, in the same way they come to you.

Health struggles.
Career changes.
Parenting, financial strain, and even the heartbreaking loss of loved ones.

Challenges like these will test you to the core. And others weigh on you daily.

Some excuses are obvious. Like that pile of mail on the counter that you keep meaning to open.

You know the one.

It's been there long enough to feel like furniture.

And other excuses hide in your good intentions, waiting for "someday."

The "someday" that somehow never becomes today.

Excuses show up everywhere.

Sometimes they're so small, you just learn to live with them. Like the missing paint on our kitchen wall.

There was a small section that was never fully painted. It was one of those "someday" excuses just weighing me down.

Just a small spot in the corner. Not many people would even notice it.

But for 6 years I walked past that wall and felt annoyed.
For 6 years, that excuse drew my eyes to that corner every day.
6 years that I wished things were different.

Until one day, soon after buying the motorhome, I decided I was done letting excuses drive my life.

I woke up.
Walked into the kitchen.
Felt the same annoyance I'd felt every day for years.
And I almost kept walking.

Almost.

But that day was different.

I stopped.

Only for a few seconds. But it was long enough to make a different choice.

I grabbed my car keys and drove to the paint store. I bought a small can of paint, went home, and just painted that annoying spot in the corner.

It took me just over an hour from the time I left to the time I set the paintbrush down. It wasn't perfect. But I've never looked at that corner the same way since.

I went to bed that night with a deep sense of relief and accomplishment.

It was such a small spot.
I had no idea how much energy it had been quietly draining until it was gone.

It might sound like such a small thing, but it changed me. It made me want to live a life of **NO EXCUSES** even more.

Here's what I've learned to expect.

Excuses will always be there. What changes is how quickly you notice them and move anyway.

Even as I wrote this book, excuses showed up countless times.

Analysis paralysis.
Perfectionism.
The feeling that nothing was ever quite ready.

There were days I didn't write a single word because I didn't know where to go next.

I was stuck.
Frustrated.
And I wanted to quit.

But of all the excuses that showed up, one was louder than the rest.

Blame.

I blamed my environment for why I couldn't think clearly or write consistently.

Every day at 2:30 p.m., when the school bell rang and my 4 kids plowed through the front door, the loudest thought hit me.

"I'll do this later. When the house is calmer."

Parents, you know exactly what I mean. And you also know how well that plan works.

I wasn't going to get a quieter house. If I wanted to write this book, I needed to get creative.

So, I parked my old-school motorhome beside my parents' house and turned it into my office.

It wasn't perfect.
Sometimes the lights glitched and sometimes the heater didn't function.

But it worked.

There's always a way to do the thing that you say matters to you.

The book that you're holding in your hands is proof that action defeats excuses.

When you notice the excuses in your day and decide you're done letting them run your life, everything changes.

You stop waiting.
And you start living.

WHY I WROTE THIS BOOK

After every keynote, people pull me aside and tell me what's really going on.

CEOs want energy back in the workplace. They want clarity and alignment as the organization grows.

Department heads want accountability that works without burnout or micromanagement.

Managers want their teams to follow through and produce consistent results.

And parents want to feel confident that they're leading their family well.

Most people think they need more motivation. But they don't.

They need ownership.
They need simple tools.
And they need small wins they can repeat.

That's why this book exists.

I wrote it for you.

HOW THIS BOOK WILL BENEFIT YOU

This book shows you how to lead yourself first.

It gives you simple tools to stop hesitating and start taking ownership when it matters most.

You'll learn how to create small wins that build real momentum. The kind that brings clarity, consistency, and confidence back into your work, your leadership, and your home.

Not just through motivation.
But through action.

60 seconds at a time.

Living with **NO EXCUSES** changed my life.

I know it will change yours too.

CONTENTS

Chapter 1: You Aren't Stuck. You're Waiting.   **21**

Shattered on Impact   21

The Gap Where Dreams Get Delayed   27

What Waiting Looks Like   30

"Mind The Gap"   34

Don't Come Back the Same   39

Chapter 2: Are You an Excuser?   **43**

But I Don't Make Excuses... Do I?   43

See it to Change it   47

The Awareness Advantage   50

The 5 Excusers   52

From Excuser to Executer   57

Chapter 3: The Friction Factor™   **61**

Let's Work Backwards   61

What Is the Friction Factor™?   65

Willpower Runs on Energy   70

Stop Skipping The Hard Part   73

Find Your Corner 4   75

Use Friction To Your Advantage   77

Chapter 4: Own Your Progress   **81**

Where You Look is Where You Go   81

Own Your Growth   89

Get Yourself Up   91

Standing at the Edge of What's Next   94

Small Choices, Big Results   98

Chapter 5: The Power of the Next 60 Seconds ... 101

The Only Minute That Counts ... 101

The Stairs Are Always Working ... 107

Which Side of Progress Are You Standing On? ... 110

When Courage Moves Faster Than Fear ... 113

Move Away from being Stuck ... 117

Chapter 6: If Nothing Changes... ... 121

Stop Blaming the Track ... 121

Nothing Changes Unless You Do ... 129

Life Without Excuses ... 131

The Power of One Thing ... 134

Be the Person Who Does the Work ... 137

Chapter 7: Purpose in Real Time ... 141

The Street Where My Olympic Dream Came Alive ... 141

No Purpose, No Progress ... 147

When Yesterday's Purpose isn't the Same as Today's ... 150

The 1-1-1 Weekly Focus ... 154

Your Life on Purpose ... 156

Chapter 8: Mercy in the Middle ... 161

A Moment I Can Never Get Back ... 161

How Mercy Shifts Your Direction ... 165

Where Mercy Matters Most ... 171

Give Yourself Permission ... 175

A Life Built on Mercy ... 179

Chapter 9: Build Consistent Results ... 183

One Foot in Front of The Other ... 183

The Power of Little Things ... 187

People Like Us Do Things Like This ... 191

The NO EXCUSES Method ... 196

Preparation is the Key to Consistency. Period. ... 200

Chapter 10: 1% Better   **203**

Simple Isn't Easy   203

Want Big Change? Start Small   208

Hidden One Percenters   212

The 1% Reset   214

Excellence Lives in the Small Stuff   217

Chapter 11: Lead in the Hallway   **223**

This Is Your Moment   223

Belief Is Contagious   226

Calm Under Pressure   230

Be Where You Are   234

When Leaders LIsten   238

Chapter 12: Live Your Legacy   **243**

This is the Moment   243

Live the Story You Want Remembered   249

The Statement That Shapes Your Story   252

The S.I.X.T.Y. Second Shift™   255

Live the Life You Want To Live   259

Acknowledgements   **263**

About The Author   **265**

CHAPTER 1

You Aren't Stuck. You're Waiting.

*"The only thing holding you back is the story
you keep telling yourself."*
—Lewis Howes

SHATTERED ON IMPACT

You always have a choice.

Even when it doesn't feel like it.

Especially when it doesn't feel like it.

Some choices shape a day. Others reshape a life. But every single one of them is still a choice.

I had no idea I would learn this lesson the hard way.

It was October 19, 2005, and I was number one in the world. The gold jersey was mine and the Olympics were 114 days away.

As I stood at the top of the icy track that I'd been down a hundred times before, I took a deep breath in.

Adrenaline rushed through me.

It was just a practice run. But I still felt that mix of nerves and thrill that comes right before you push off the starting block.

Here's the thing.

Skeleton racing looks like mayhem from the outside. There aren't many people who would willingly sprint at full speed, dive onto their stomach on a thin sheet of metal, and slide down an ice chute at 90 miles per hour with their chin an inch from the track.

When people watch the sport of skeleton, they see sheer chaos and assume survival is the goal.

But to me, skeleton racing feels like freedom.

It's a dance choreographed by gravity.

Timing.
Rhythm.
Precision.

Each movement connected to the other. And if one thing is off, everything is.

Every sacrifice, every mile away from home, and every drop of sweat was finally paying off.

It was day one of training for our U.S. Olympic trials, and it was my turn to go.

I pushed off the start and slid down the track. Steering my way in and out of every corner. It was a beautiful run. A really fast one. The kind of run that makes you believe the season is already written.

I crossed the finish line and waited at the finish dock like always.

My breathing slowed and the excitement built inside me. My times were proving that I was about to become an Olympian.

As I waited for the truck to pick me up and take me back up the mountain, I couldn't help but think of my bright future ahead.

I smiled.
Closed my eyes.
Took in a deep breath and slowly let it out.

And that's when I heard it.

A low rumbling sound that didn't make sense. It should've been the soft hum of my teammate's sled gliding across the ice.

But it wasn't.

A 4-man bobsled had been sent down the track without warning, and the brakes were never pulled.

I looked over my shoulder just in time to see it coming. 1400 pounds of steel barreling straight toward me at 70 miles an hour.

It happened so fast.

I didn't even have time to think. It was just a blur of noise and fear.

I took a step to jump out of the way of its path.

But it was too late.

The bobsled flew out of the track and hit me from behind.

The impact lifted me off the ground.
I was thrown 25 feet and slammed onto the asphalt.
My thoughts immediately raced.

"What just happened!? How did I end up here?"

I tried to stand, but my body collapsed beneath me.

I couldn't run away.
I couldn't crawl.
I couldn't even hold my own weight.

I looked down, trying to understand what just happened. Why wouldn't my body do what it had done a million times before?

And that's when I saw it.

My right foot was twisted backward with my heel pressing against my calf.

The bones were sticking out of my leg.

In a split second, my body and my dreams were shattered.

The world went silent, and the air felt too thick to breathe. It was one of those moments when everything slows down and time stops existing.

Sometimes, time stands still when you celebrate a major event. Like when you hold your newborn for the first time. When you say "I do." Or when you sign the deal, you thought would never close.

You've experienced this, right?

When life's so good that you're unaware of time passing by around you?

Ya, it was like that.
But opposite.

Every bump in the ambulance felt like a hammer to my leg. I tried to stay conscious, but the pain took over.

When I woke up from surgery and saw the damage to my leg, I felt my heart break into a million pieces. The reality of what this injury meant for my future hit me even harder than the crash.

I bet you've had a day like this too.

When life delivers a hit so hard you just want to rewind. Pretend it didn't happen. Go back to how things used to be.

Those days don't just test you. They transform you.

THE ROOM OF DOUBT AND FEAR

The hospital staff called it a recovery room. But it felt like a prison for my body and my mind.

The beeping monitors. The smell of antiseptic. The hum of the lights above me.

I had nowhere to go and nothing to do but think. And the thoughts came fast.

How did this happen? Why now? What about everything I've worked for?

The pain wasn't just in my leg. It was in my chest. My throat. My spine. And it held me captive. My identity had been built on movement, speed, and strength. And now I couldn't even lift myself out of bed.

At that moment, the voice in my head got loud.

"The gold jersey is gone. It's over for you."

Everything would be different now and each doubt that swirled in my mind whispered the same message.

"You'll never be the same."

Lying there, it felt like my life had stopped. Like I was stuck in that bed, stuck in that body, stuck in a future I didn't choose. But looking back, I wasn't stuck.

I was waiting.

Waiting for the pain to ease. Waiting for answers. Waiting for someone else to tell me what came next.

I tried to be strong. I really did. But the pain broke through, and the tears began to flow.

Right then, the hospital door flew open and my surgeon stormed in with a clipboard in hand. Her timing was impeccable.

No smile.
No sugarcoating.

She walked in with purpose, like she had something important to tell me about the surgery. But when she saw the tears on my face, she stopped in her tracks. Whatever she had planned to say disappeared.

She looked straight at me, tilted her head, and asked, *"Why are you crying?"*

I just stared in disbelief.

So, she said it again.
Slowly.

"Why are you crying?"

I didn't answer. How could I?

So, she kept going.

"Listen. You can look back and be miserable about what happened. Or you can move forward. Your leg is broken. And feeling sorry for yourself won't change that. You choose."

Her words cut through the air like a scalpel. And the door slammed on her way out.

I think I sat in shock for the next hour trying to process the scene.

I didn't realize it then, but she wasn't being cruel. She was being clear. She wasn't only trying to fix my leg but she was trying to help me fix my mind. I mean, it was a roundabout way of doing it, for sure.

But it worked.

That moment became a mirror moment in my life. She handed me a truth that I didn't want to face.

She reminded me that I could keep replaying what I lost. Or I could start rebuilding what I had left.

It took time for those words to settle, but I've never forgotten the message.

"Noelle, you ALWAYS have a choice."

Day by day. Choice by choice. I came back.
Physically. Mentally. Emotionally.

I fought through sadness, doubt, blame, depression, and pain. But the lesson from that hospital room kept echoing in my mind.

Just like my doctor told me on that cold night in October, I'm telling you now.

You always have a choice.

Stop blaming your circumstances or listening to doubt like it knows the truth. The moment you own your choices, the weight of *what if* turns into the power of *what's next.*

Harvey Cox said it best.

"Not to decide is to decide."

You can choose to do something or choose not to. But staying stuck is still a decision. It's the one that keeps you right where you are.

The absolute, non-negotiable hard truth is this.

Inaction is the easiest and most destructive choice you make every single day.

THE GAP WHERE DREAMS GET DELAYED

You already know what you need to do to make more money, get in shape, and upskill. But actually, doing it is a different story.

You know what I'm talking about.

You buy the mulch.
You set the bags in the yard.
You even Google "best way to edge flower beds."

And 3 weeks later, the mulch is still sitting in the driveway, half the grass is dead, and every time you walk past it, you tell yourself, *"I'll get to it this weekend."*

There's a name for this.

Behavioral science calls it the **Intention-Action Gap.**

It's the place where you write your goals in your note's app, feel motivated for about ten minutes, and then never take the first step to make any of them real.

That's the gap.

It shows up in tiny moments, but it's deceptively powerful. Because it's not a place where you fail. At least failure teaches you something. This gap is far worse.

It's a place of waiting.

It's where excuses rush in and dreams get delayed.

This territory is home to what I call **The 5 Excusers.**

The Blamer. The Doubter. The Avoider. The Pleaser. The Justifier.

The Excusers live in the gap between intention and action. I'll introduce each one of the 5 in the next chapter and show you exactly how their excuses keep you stuck. But for now, let's take a look at what those Excusers keep us from doing.

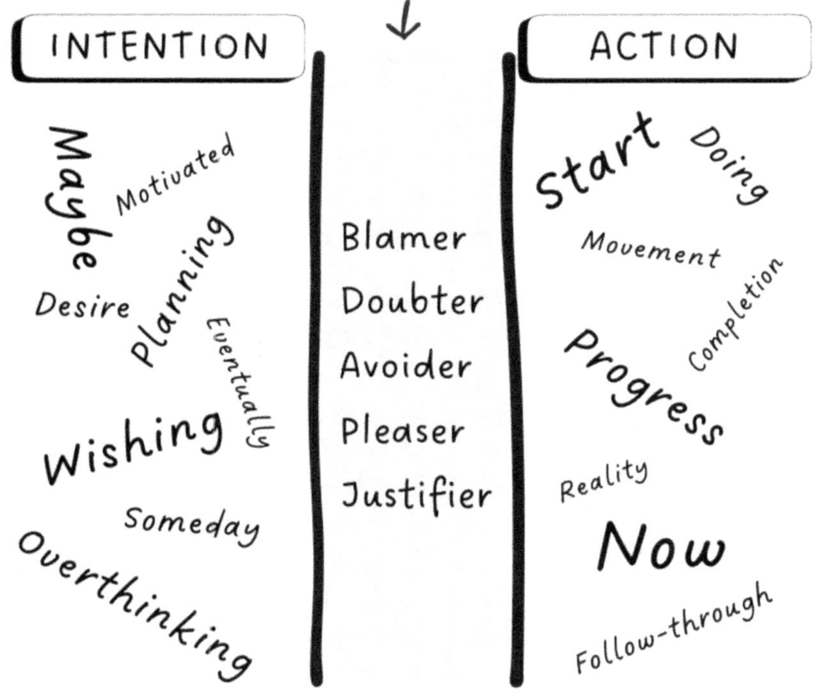

Think of it this way.

You decide it's time for a vacation. You deserve it. You intend to go. You open your phone and start searching flights, scrolling through pictures of beaches, mountains, or maybe Paris.

You're not sure yet.

Then the questions start.

Do you want basic, economy, or premium? Window or aisle? Add a bag? Upgrade legroom?

Suddenly your dream getaway feels like a pop quiz.

You finally see a great deal, but the dates overlap with 2 appointments and your kid's soccer game.

So, you sigh, close the app, and tell yourself you'll wait until next week. But you don't. You never take action on your intention.

I literally did this last week.

Too many options, no clear plan, and your purpose gets buried under pop-up distractions.

You say you want "more success," "better health," or "more significant relationships," but without a better plan, you can't take off. You avoid, doubt or justify your way into inaction.

But here's the simple truth.

All it takes is a quick burst of action.

A plane can't leave the runway without speed. Neither can you. Sometimes you just need to take off and then figure out the destination in the air.

The good news?

Bridging the gap from intention to action can happen really fast.

60 seconds fast.

If you want better health, stretch your body between meetings. You don't need a full workout. You just need to move.

If you want more success, do the most important thing on your list today. Not all of it. Just the one that actually matters.

Want stronger relationships? Send one text that says, "Thinking of you." That's it.

And here's a great tip. When you decide ahead of time exactly *when* and *where* you'll act, you're far more likely to follow through.

This is what effective leaders do. They create a plan before excuses show up.

'When I get to the office, I'll file 3 reports before opening the email.'

No debate. No delay. Just action.

The space between who you are and who you want to be isn't filled with luck or circumstances. The life you want or don't want is built by the choices you make.

But comfort is sneaky. And it loves to take the wheel.

It whispers thing like, *"I'm tired. I'll start tomorrow."*

It convinces you that waiting is safer than moving. And before you know it, the days all blur together. Another year passes, and nothing has really changed.

If this feels familiar, you're not alone. Comfort has a way of making capable people drift.

Let me show you what this looks like.

I want to introduce you to someone.

Meet Bob.

WHAT WAITING LOOKS LIKE

Bob isn't a bad guy.

He's a decent coworker, flosses when he remembers, and sometimes gives his neighbor a half nod to say "hey."

But Bob is a professional excuse maker.

He thinks he's stuck. But he's not. He's just waiting in "the gap" and hoping things will change.

Today is no different.

It starts with 3 rounds of snooze.

He stayed up late Googling "how to get rich without doing much," so now the morning is his enemy. He grabs his phone to check the weather, but forty minutes later, he still doesn't know if it'll rain.

Now he's late and breakfast is a lost cause.

Stressed, he rushes to work, bursts through the office doors and shouts, *"It wasn't my fault!"*

Traffic. City planners. Somehow his wife, for buying a house "too far from work."

By the time Bob reaches his desk, his brain feels like a pinball machine.

Emails. Meetings. Notifications.

He doesn't plan his day. He reacts to it. Poorly.

A coworker asks about the project deadline. Bob sighs.

"Yeah, I'd be done if people would stop interrupting me."

He spends the next hour scrolling headlines and checking fantasy football scores.

When his spouse texts him to grab milk, he sends an immediate text back.

"What am I, your assistant?"

He regrets it, but not enough to apologize.

He leaves the office early without telling anyone, logs a full day, and ignores the follow-up he promised to send.

On the drive home, every red light feels personal. Every slow driver feels like an insult.

When he walks through the door and trips over his daughter's shoes, he snaps.

Bob blames his family for his problems, retreats to the basement, and disappears into Netflix.

That night, he lies in bed, one arm across his forehead like he's in a dramatic movie scene.

He wonders why he feels so stuck. And he doubts things could ever really change.

Then his daughter tiptoes in and whispers, *"Daddy, are you mad at me?"*

Her eyes hold concern. And love.

The question lands like a punch wrapped in a hug. Because deep down, Bob knows the truth.

He's not mad at her.
He's mad at himself.

Mad at the excuses.
Mad at the drifting.
Mad that he keeps waiting for life to make the calls.

He falls asleep thinking, *"I don't want to live like this anymore."*

WHAT CHOOSING LOOKS LIKE

When the alarm goes off that next morning, Bob feels it.

That brief hesitation between wanting and doing. It takes place in less than 60 seconds, but those seconds hold the power to change a day.

And this time he chooses to cross the gap.

He sits up. Groggy, but up.

He stretches for 30 seconds and says out loud, *"This is my day. I'm choosing it."*

No fireworks. No motivational playlist. Just ownership.

He skips the scroll. Cooks eggs. And leaves 5 minutes early.

Traffic is still slow, but this time he listens to an audiobook instead of rehearsing complaints.

He arrives refreshed and on time.

At work, nothing has magically changed.

The inbox is still full.
The client is still demanding.
The coworker still complains.

But Bob pauses before reacting. He breathes. He focuses on what he can control.

One report.
Then the next.

When Lisa asks about the project, he doesn't dodge or defend.

"I dropped the ball," he says. *"I've got it now."*

She smiles.
No drama.
Just accountability.

At lunch, he walks around the building instead of scrolling.

When his spouse texts about scheduling the car repair, he replies, *"Got it. Love you."*

No sarcasm. No sigh. Just kindness.

By the afternoon, he's tired. But he's proud.

When he gets home, his kids are loud, and his wife looks worn out.

He hugs her.
Listens.
Helps with dinner.

Nothing about his life looks dramatically different.

Same job.
Same traffic.
Same distractions.

But Bob didn't change his whole life.

He just changed one minute of it.
Then another.
And by the end of the day, those minutes changed him.

Bob stopped waiting around. And he climbed out of the gap.

"MIND THE GAP"

If you've ever been on the London Underground, you've heard the phrase, *"Mind the gap."*

It's a simple safety warning.

Watch the space between the platform and the train.

But in life, there's another gap that's just as dangerous.
The space between what you intend to do and what you actually do.

Between goals and results.
Promises and follow-through.
Words and action.

And almost every dream that dies quietly does so right here.

The gap is where people say they're stuck. But nothing is actually holding them back.

They're just waiting.

Waiting for clarity. Waiting for confidence. Waiting for life to feel easier before they move.

You've been here. Or maybe you're here now.

You tell yourself you'll start tomorrow, reach out later, or decide when things calm down. And before you know it, the gap between who you are and who you could be gets wider.

It's not that you don't care. It's that you don't move.

You're waiting for a magical hot air balloon to carry you to the other side of your goals, when what you really need are the tools to build a bridge to get you there.

So, let's pull out the toolbox.

Take a look at this example.

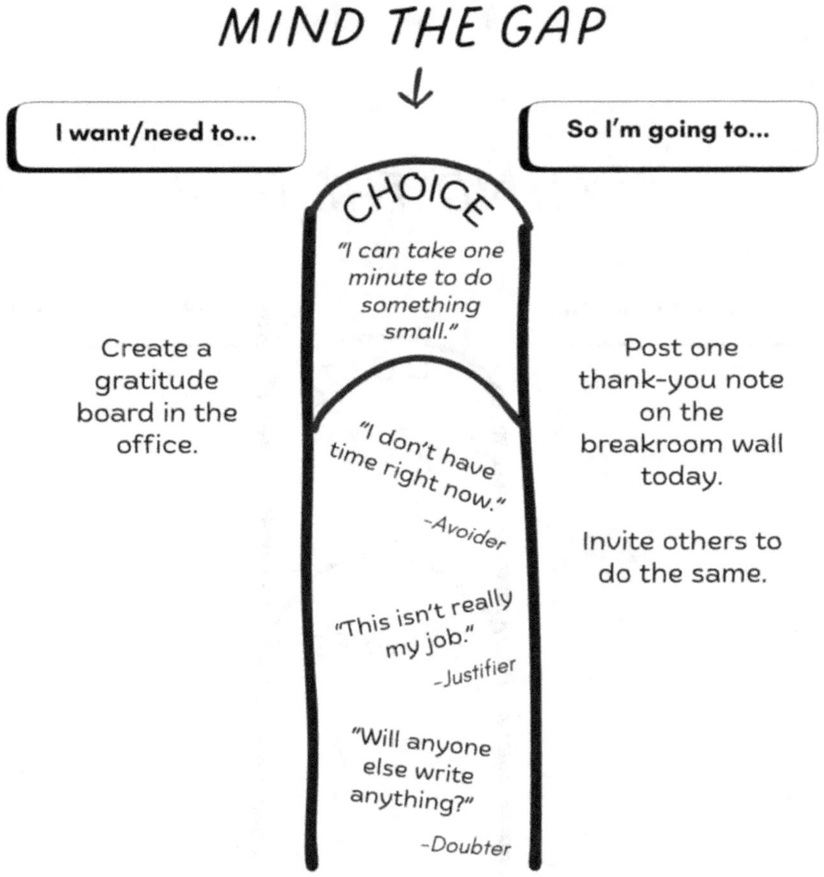

This is your life right now. There are 2 sides. On the left is intention. On the right is action. And in the middle is the place where most people get stuck. The gap. The pause. The excuses.

The bridge across that gap is choice.

In the example, notice how simple it is.

One intention. One clear choice in the middle. One specific action on the other side.

No motivation required. No perfect plan. Just ownership.

Now it's your turn to build your bridge using what I call the **3 Tools of Ownership**.

Notice. Decide. Act.

Grab a piece of paper or use the space provided.

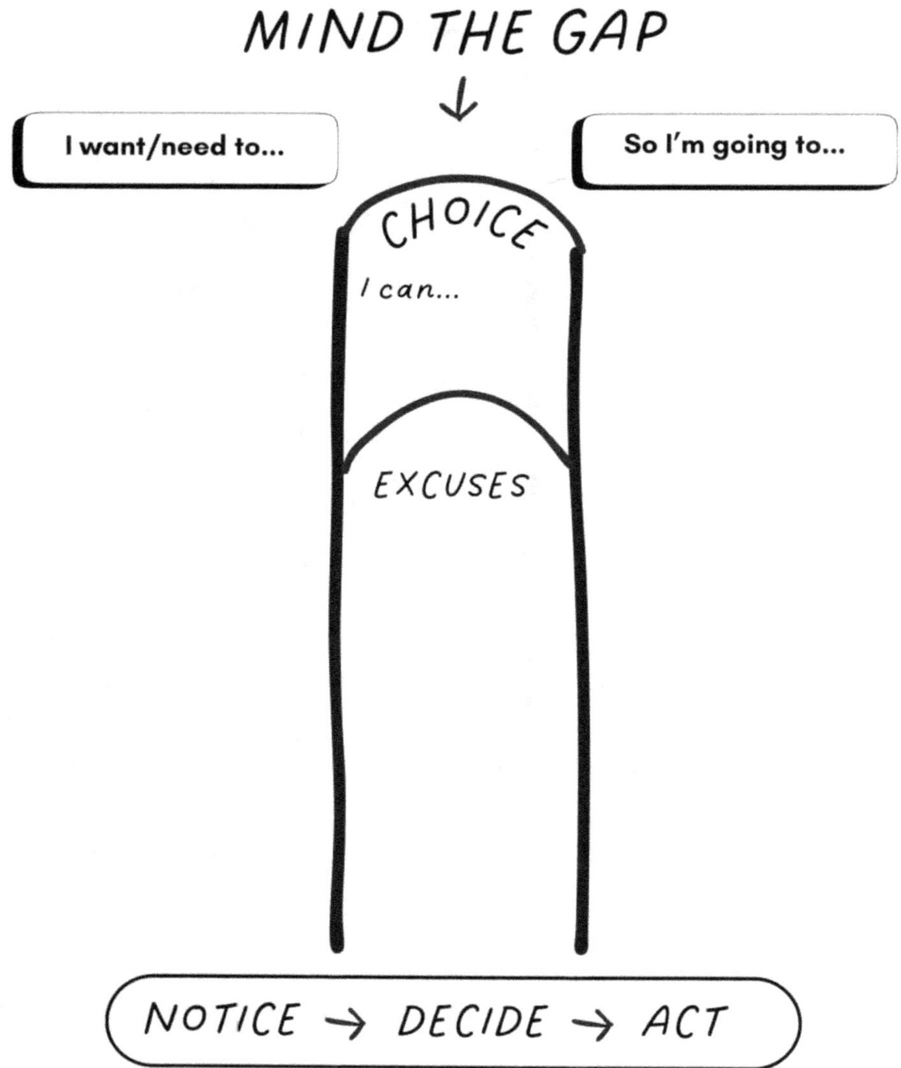

Step 1: Notice

Start on the left side.

Under **"I want or need to..."**, write one thing you've been intending to do.

Just one.

The thing you keep thinking about.
The task you keep stepping around.
The conversation you keep saying you'll get to later.

Write it down.

If nothing jumps out right away, give yourself a minute.

Maybe you want to set clear priorities each day, give feedback to an employee or finally sign up for that program that's been sitting in your bookmarks. Maybe you want to start an exercise program or create that gratitude board you've been talking about.

This step is about awareness. And awareness is always where change starts.

Step 2: Decide

Now look at the space in the middle.

This is the gap.

This is where hesitation lives. Where excuses sneak in. And where most people wait.

But you're not going to wait. You're going to decide what's possible and choose to take a small step forward.

On the bridge, write one sentence that starts with this.

"I can..."

Not what you *should* do. Not what you *wish* you'd do. But what you *can* do.

I can take one minute.
I can send one message.
I can clear one surface.
I can do one set.

Small counts.

When you realize the choice really is yours and that it can be something so small, your brain tells you it's possible.

<u>Step 3: Act</u>

Now move to the right side.

Under **"So I'm going to…"**, write one clear action.

Not someday.
Today.

Make it specific.
Make it small.
Make it doable.

When you define the action, your brain stops negotiating and starts moving.

Set the alarm. Send the text. Pull out the hammer and 3 nails. Take the first step. It doesn't need to be perfect. It just needs to happen. And when the action is clear, you move over your excuses, and they no longer control you.

You'll stand at this gap **every day.** Between intention and action.

When you feel the pause, that's your signal.

Use the **3 Tools of Ownership.**

Notice. Decide. Act.

Because choice is the bridge between where you are and where you actually want to go.

DON'T COME BACK THE SAME

Lying in my hospital recovery room, one thought kept repeating.

"You'll never be the same."

And I was right.
But not in the way I expected.

The accident pushed me more than I could have imagined.
My body.
My mind.
Me.

I wanted to be the same person I used to be. But through it all, I learned something simple. We shouldn't want to stay the same. Experience is what brings meaning to life. The point of it is to grow.

I came back better and faster than before. But the real change wasn't physical. It was in how I took ownership of my life.

I stopped drifting through decisions. I paid attention to the gaps. I noticed where excuses liked to hide. And even on the hardest days, I chose to cross the bridge anyway.

My husband built my Olympic sled. My children traveled by my side. And when we arrived at the Olympic Games in Sochi, Russia, it felt like something bigger than a comeback.

It was proof.

Proof that the limits we fear are often the ones we've never tested.

When you do the thing, you didn't believe you could do, it rewrites what you believe is possible.

LET IT CHANGE YOU

There's a name for what happens when pain transforms you instead of paralyzing you. Psychologists call it post-traumatic growth.

I call it a choice.

The most difficult challenges don't just test individuals. They shape teams. They define cultures. They clarify a purpose. This is true in life and in business.

Take Starbucks, for example.

In 2008, Howard Schultz returned as CEO during one of the company's lowest points.

Stores were closing. Quality was slipping. The culture had lost its edge.

Schultz didn't try to plow forward. Instead, he shut every store down for retraining.

Not to fix coffee. But to refocus on people.

"We're not in the coffee business serving people," he said. *"We're in the people business serving coffee."*

Adversity gave Starbucks the chance to reinvent. And that choice saved the brand.

That same opportunity exists inside every challenge you face.
The question isn't whether it's there. It's whether you'll take it.

THE REWARD ON THE OTHER SIDE

When you finally move past your excuses and take action, your life starts to change in ways you can feel.

Your mind feels lighter because you stopped carrying guilt. The pressure releases from your chest. You sleep better because you earned your rest.

Your jeans fit better.
The fence post gets fixed.
The gratitude board finally goes up.

And one morning, you catch your reflection and realize something quietly powerful.

You like who you see.

Not because life is perfect. But because you're keeping promises to yourself.

Viktor Frankl said it best.

"When we are no longer able to change a situation, we are challenged to change ourselves."

That's the invitation hidden inside every setback. But it has to be *your* decision.

You *ALWAYS* have a choice.

So, stop waiting.

You can replay what broke you. Or you can choose to focus on what builds you.

Start where you are.
Not where you were.
Not where you wish you'd started a year ago.

Climb out of the gap.

Start with one thing you've been meaning to do.
Take one step today.

And when life hands you your own bobsled moments, the ones that stretch you and shatter you, here's my advice.

Don't come back the same.

You're not supposed to.

CHAPTER 2

Are You an Excuser?

"Successful people have the same problems you do.
They just stop making excuses for them."
—James Clear

BUT I DON'T MAKE EXCUSES... DO I?

I had just graduated high school when I received the invitation to train with the national bobsled and skeleton teams in Lake Placid, New York. It was a dream come true.

The day I arrived, I put on my gym clothes and walked to the weight room. The energy hit me before I even opened the door.

Techno music blasted through the air. Barbells slammed against the floor. Shouts of encouragement ricocheted between the walls. The sounds vibrated like thunder, and the room pulsed with adrenaline.

Every instinct told me to turn around and walk away.

Looking back, I can now see that it was a clue that I was being an excuser.

You've been there, haven't you?

You say you want the opportunity, the promotion, or the change, but when the chance comes, something inside you keeps you from moving towards it.

I stepped to the edge of the gym doorway, looked in, and immediately froze.

That weight room didn't just test strength. It exposed confidence. Every inch of that room radiated discipline and intensity. And the Olympic rings were everywhere. They were painted on the walls. The floors. The weight racks. You couldn't miss them.

Every rep had power.
Every lift had purpose.
And then there was me.

No plan.
No program.
No idea what I was doing.

Just standing there thinking, *"Maybe I should stretch first."*

I was the youngest one there and everyone around me looked like they'd been sculpted by the gods. I'm not exaggerating. The athletes looked like marble statues that came to life.

Shoulders like armor. Abs sculpted by Michelangelo. Legs that could outrun lightning itself. Their bodies would make Zeus proud.

These athletes carried themselves with the confidence of champions. And I carried my water bottle like it might protect me.

Every person in that weight room belonged there. And I did not.

I didn't want to walk in and get corrected, or worse, get yelled at. So, I told myself I'd go later. When it was quiet. When I felt ready.

I thought I was being smart.

Waiting. Planning. Preparing.

For the first few days, I didn't lift a thing. I just stood in the doorway, watching the warriors inside.

I told myself I was just "getting a feel for it."

But I wasn't. I was hiding.

At lunch, when everyone else was eating, I'd sneak in and wander around the gym. If someone g anced in, I pretended I was looking for something.

Please. I wasn't looking for anything. I just didn't know what to do.

One morning, I finally got up the courage to walk in while others were training. I tucked myself beside the medicine balls, hoping no one would notice me.

I looked to the athletes on my left. Then I looked to the ones on my right. And I just started copying whatever they were doing.

If they did squats, I did squats. If they did push press, I attempted push press. If they started juggling barbells, I probably would have tried that too.

I wasn't training. I was performing.

Then, it happened.

Mid-lunge, I caught my reflection in the mirror. The athlete next to me looked strong, steady, and confident.

I didn't.

My shoulders were uneven, my form was off, and my face said it all. I didn't look like an athlete. I looked like someone pretending to be one. I was embarrassed and had to look away.

That's when it struck me.

The mirror didn't just show me my form. It showed me the truth. I wasn't afraid of hard work. I was afraid of what others thought of me. I thought I had to prove I belonged in that gym, instead of actually believing I already did.

That's what excuses really are. Camouflage for insecurity. They mask the cracks in our self-confidence like a band-aid over a bullet hole.

Self-awareness always shows up in a quiet moment. And most of the time, we rush right past it. Too busy. Too distracted. Too afraid to look closer.

Standing in that gym, I finally saw the truth. And it was painful to see.

My excuses weren't protecting me. They were actually trapping me. I was sick of feeling so lost and insecure. So, I finally decided to do something about it.

One thing. Something so small.
I sent an email.

That was it. Less than 60 seconds. One question.

"Can you create a workout plan for me?"

The response came back that afternoon. *"Absolutely."*

By that evening, I had hired a strength and conditioning coach. Someone to teach me. Push me. Hold me accountable.

And you know what happened?

That one action crushed the excuses I had created in my mind. Because now I had a plan. I had a program. I had an idea of what I needed to do each day. And all I could think was, *"Why didn't I do this sooner?"*

That's the cost of excuses. They cost you energy and time. And you always realize later how small the first step actually was.

I wasn't the fastest.
I wasn't the strongest.
And I definitely didn't have abs sculpted by Michelangelo.
In fact, I usually lifted the least amount of weight in the room.

But I showed up.

And every time I did, confidence met me there.

SEE YOURSELF CLEARLY

Awareness changes everything. It changes how you think. How you lead. How you live.

The moment you stop lying to yourself, the gap between knowing and doing starts to close. Not all at once. But one honest moment at a time.

That's where progress actually begins.

Because when you see yourself clearly, you stop fighting imaginary problems and start facing the real ones. You can finally name what's slowing you down. And once you can name it, you can move past it.

Clarity creates choice. Choice creates change. And it all starts with awareness.

SEE IT TO CHANGE IT

Picture a mirror fogged with steam after a hot shower.

My mirror doesn't just reflect me. It reflects 4 kids who clearly think steam is the best art medium ever invented.

As you look at the foggy mirror, you know your reflection is there, but you can't see it clearly.

That's what excuses do. They cloud the truth. They blur your reflection until all you can make out are outlines of potential.

You wipe and wipe, but the fog keeps coming back because the source is still running. Your habits. Your stories. Your distractions.

Awareness is the moment you finally realize you don't need to wipe harder. You need to turn off the steam. It's when you stop trying to see *around* the fog and decide to clear it. Only then can you see yourself as you really are.

THE MIRROR MOMENT EXERCISE

If you want to become someone you've never been, you have to be willing to get uncomfortable.

The only way an athlete improves is by practicing outside of their comfort zone. And self-awareness is no different.

When you practice self-awareness, you raise your standards. You sharpen your focus. You start living like the person you say you want to be.

So, let's practice.

For this exercise you'll need 2 things:

1. A mirror.
2. A timer set for 60 seconds.

Find a mirror. Any mirror. If you don't have a mirror nearby, open the camera on your phone and put it on selfie mode.

Now here's what you're going to do.

Look yourself in the eyes. Just you and your reflection.

No fidgeting. No fixing your hair. No judging your outfit.

This isn't about your looks. This is about what's going on beneath the surface.

Don't worry if someone's watching. Don't wonder what they're thinking.

Just look at your reflection.

When the timer begins, hold eye contact and ask yourself this question:

What am I pretending not to see each day?

The doubts. The comparisons. The fear, judgment or pride.

The excuses.

What's hiding from your view?

Now choose an area in your life to think about.

Your career.
Your health.
Your marriage.
As a parent.

With your finances, your time or in your relationships with friends or co-workers.

Your mind will want to look away. It's normal. That's discomfort talking.

Stay with it and keep eye contact.

Are you ready?

Ask yourself, *"What am I pretending not to see each day?"*

Now start your 60-second timer and look at yourself. It's time to reflect.

...

...

...

That's it. You felt that.

A word surfaced. A face flashed. A habit showed up. And even if you tried to push it away, you knew. It's time to turn off the steam. It's time to change.

This is what awareness feels like. It's raw, revealing, and unfiltered.

You can't live with **NO EXCUSES** if you're unwilling to look at yourself honestly.

Most people can't make it the full minute.

They look away. They fidget. They laugh it off.

That's fear doing its job.

But if you stay with it, something shifts and you start *seeing* yourself clearly.

Imagine what would change if you did this once a day.

MIRROR MOMENT: THE 7-DAY CHALLENGE

Choose one mirror that you look into every day. The bathroom mirror. The car visor. The gym. That's your reflection point. Each day, when you see yourself in that mirror, pause for one simple question that will remove the fog.

"What does NO EXCUSES look like today?"

Do this for 7 days, and you'll start to notice patterns you've been too busy to see. How you spend your time. Where you avoid discomfort. When you drift into distraction. You'll catch yourself in moments of hesitation and begin to choose differently.

A small, consistent moment of honesty compounds into big results.

Keep showing up to that mirror. Be honest with yourself. One day at a time. One look at a time. And you'll prove to yourself that change is possible.

FACE TO FACE WITH CHANGE

Here's the truth about that mirror.

It's not magic. It's your brain.

When you stop looking away, your choices begin to line up with your values.

Psychologists call this self-concordance.
I like to call it alignment.

It's the moment when who you *are* finally lines up with who you *say* you want to be. And every time you look in the mirror without judging yourself, your brain learns something powerful.

You're safe. You can tell the truth. And you can change.

THE AWARENESS ADVANTAGE

Dr. Tal Ben-Shahar, creator of Harvard's world-famous course on Positive Psychology, teaches that self-awareness is the first step to growth.

"You cannot improve what you don't understand," he often said.

He's right.

Change begins the moment you stop looking away. It begins when you take the time to understand what's really getting in the way of your progress.

Self-awareness is the foundation of improvement. It increases empathy, reduces stress, and improves well-being. It's what makes us human.

And while technology can process information faster than we ever could, it can't do what self-awareness does.

AI can describe behavior, but self-awareness is what allows us to change it.

AI CAN'T REPLACE THIS

I was recently in a meeting with leaders from NiCE, a global AI-powered cloud company that serves more than 150 countries and over 80 of the Fortune 100.

I was impressed.

For a company built on artificial intelligence, their focus isn't on the tech. It's on the people behind it.

They asked me to help their teams strengthen awareness. Not just awareness of their work, but awareness of themselves.

They want employees who look in the mirror, notice where they need to improve, and take the initiative to do something about it.

Their priority is clear.

They're building a culture of ownership.
Ownership of growth.
Ownership of learning.
Ownership of self.

The world is upgrading faster than we can download the updates. And they don't want people waiting to be told what to improve.

They want people who notice first.

Their leaders understand something most companies miss.

Technology may power progress. But people sustain it. And awareness is the foundation of every meaningful change.

SOMETHING IN YOUR TEETH

Think of it this way.

Awareness is that friend who tells you you've got spinach in your teeth.

It's uncomfortable for about 2 seconds.

But that moment of truth saves you from walking around all day pretending everything's fine.

The truth stings.
But it also frees you.

Eckhart Tolle put it this way.

"Awareness is the greatest agent for change. The moment you become aware of something, you are no longer trapped in it."

When you bring awareness to fear, anger, or resistance, those emotions lose their grip. You stop identifying with them and you're able to release them.

When you start paying attention to your thoughts and choices every day, something shifts.

You start catching excuses **as they happen.**

They show up in your words.
Your calendar.
The little promises you quietly break to yourself.

Every excuse has a root.

Fear. Control. Worry. Comfort.

Different roots. Same results.

You stay stuck.

Want to change your habits?

Start by noticing the excuse before it finishes the sentence.

THE 5 EXCUSERS

Let me ask you something.

If your life were a car, who's actually driving it right now?

And don't say "me," because if you're anything like the rest of us, you've got at least 5 loud, obnoxious, uninvited backseat drivers shouting directions at you every single day.

They climb in when you're tired.
When you're unsure.
When you hesitate for even one second.

And suddenly, instead of driving toward the life you want, you're dodging potholes, arguing with imaginary passengers and making wrong turns because someone in the back yelled, "STOP!" at the worst possible moment.

I call these passengers **The 5 Excusers.**

They're not who you are.
They're not your identity.
They're patterns. Thought habits. Mental hitchhikers.

They grab the wheel, shout directions, and insist they know the best route to your goals. They tell you to turn around, slow down, or pull over until the danger passes. And none of them even have a license.

And unless you can name them, they'll keep grabbing the wheel and steering your life into the same old ruts.

Ready to meet them?

Buckle up.

1. The Blamer. The One Kicking the Back of Your Seat.

The Blamer is loud. And they are constantly complaining.

If you miss a turn, it's the GPS's fault. If you're late, it's the traffic. If you stall out, it's the car manufacturer.

They never hold the wheel, but they always have someone else to blame for why you're not where you want to be.

Traffic. Weather.
Your boss. Your schedule.
Your DNA. Your childhood. Your dog.

The Blamer doesn't show up because *you're* a bad person. The Blamer shows up because your brain gets scared.

Because if it's not your fault, then it's not your responsibility. And if it's not your responsibility, then you never have to change.

The Blamer keeps you stuck by convincing you you're powerless.

2. The Avoider. The Fake Sleeper in the Backseat.

The Avoider is very quiet and they love to delay.

They're the one rummaging through the snack bag whenever a hard choice shows up. You need directions and they're elbows-deep in pretzels.

They whisper things like *"I'll start tomorrow," "I'm not ready yet,"* or my personal favorite, *"Let me clean the floor mats first."* Because with the Avoider in the car, doing *anything* is better than doing what actually needs to be done.

Avoiders make you feel "busy" while you're driving in circles.

If you've ever opened 17 tabs, color-coded your calendar, researched productivity apps, and still haven't started the actual task.

That was the Avoider.

And they're sprawled across the backseat, counting on the car to drive itself.

3. The Justifier. The Smooth Talker With a Story.

Ah, the Justifier.

They always have a "good reason."

They convince you to take the scenic route even though you're already late.

They justify stopping at every drive-thru, running every errand, and delaying every real step forward because "you deserve a break" or "it's harmless to skip it once."

And the Justifier loves distractions.

You'll pick up your phone to check the weather and somehow end up on TikTok watching a guy build a canoe out of hot glue because you have a camping trip this summer and suddenly that feels urgent.

Meanwhile, you're drifting past small promises you made to yourself and missing the exits to your dreams.

The Justifier doesn't yell.
They don't panic.
They don't fight.

They use logic. Emotional logic.

Justifiers make excuses sound reasonable and distractions seem logical. This is why they're the most dangerous passenger in your car.

The Justifier isn't lazy. They're just loyal to your comfort zone.

4. The Doubter. The One Grabbing the Panic Handle.

You know the Doubter.

They flinch every time you change lanes. They gasp at green lights. And they warn you about things that aren't happening.

"What if this doesn't work?"
"Are you sure you should do that?"
"Everything went wrong last time. Remember?"

Doubters rehearse disaster.

They think they're protecting you. They think they're helping. But their fear makes you drive like someone who doesn't trust themselves.

The Doubter's voice gets especially loud after failure.

One setback or one disappointment and suddenly they're narrating every possible worst-case scenario like a true-crime podcaster.

Doubt doesn't keep you safe. It keeps you from even starting the car and moving toward the life you actually want to live.

5. The Pleaser. The One Rewriting Your GPS for Everyone Else.

I'll be honest. This one frequently runs the show in my car.

The Pleaser turns your life into an emotional Uber ride.

You're driving the car, paying for the gas, and somehow still taking everyone else where *they* want to go. This Excuser is the overly helpful passenger who keeps offering to change your destination based on what *other people* want.

"Oh, they sighed? I'll change the entire plan."

"Oh, he looked mildly disappointed? Better cancel everything I was excited about."

One text with a sad-face emoji and the Pleaser is pulling an illegal U-turn.

Yep. This one is in my passenger seat.

Pleasers redirect your entire route so that no one feels uncomfortable, except you.

They say yes to protect feelings.
They say yes to avoid conflict.
They say yes because they believe everyone else's needs matter more.

But here's the truth.

You can't become who you want to be while steering your life around someone else's roadmap.

The Pleaser's exhaustion comes from pretending kindness is always compliance.

WHO'S ACTUALLY DRIVING?

Okay. Let's get real.

These 5 passengers will always try to climb into your mind. They'll always try to shout directions. They'll always try to take control of your life the second you hesitate.

But here's the part that changes everything.

You're the one in the driver's seat.

You choose which voice gets volume. You choose when to pull over, kick them out, and start driving again.

Your excuses are loud, but your identity is louder. So, ask yourself the only question that matters right now:

Who's driving your life today? You, or one of the 5?

It's time to take back the wheel.

FROM EXCUSER TO EXECUTER

The moment you notice an Excuser, the clock starts ticking. You have about 60 seconds to take the wheel back, or else they'll be sure to hijack your car.

And that awareness?
That's what gives you the power to shift from excusing to executing.

Hal Elrod said it best:

"The moment you take responsibility for everything in your life is the moment you can change anything in your life."

If you want to improve your life, take ownership of your thoughts.
Your words.
Your actions.

That's the moment you start living with **NO EXCUSES.**

So, let's talk about how to turn that ownership into action.

BUILD THE SYSTEM, NOT THE STORY

"You don't rise to the level of your goals. You fall to the level of your systems."
James Clear said that, and he nailed it.

Change doesn't happen because you want it more. It happens because you know what to do when excuses show up.

So instead of overthinking it, here's the move.

Remember the **3 Tools of Ownership** from chapter one? Use them.

1. **Notice.**
2. **Decide.**
3. **Act.**

That's it.

Start by noticing the thought. Notice the intention. Notice the excuse trying to slow you down.

Then what's true? Decide what's actually in your control. Decide what you can do next.

Finally, act with purpose. Take action. Even if it's small.

That's how awareness turns into execution.

Now that you can recognize the 5 Excusers, you'll start catching them in real time.

And every time you notice, decide, and act, something shifts.

You stop explaining. You stop negotiating. And you start moving.

Because the excuses no longer get to decide the direction of your life.

THE MOMENT YOU MOVE

That mirror in the Lake Placid weight room didn't just show me my form. It showed me my fear. I didn't look strong. I looked uncertain.

But the moment I **noticed** the excuse, something shifted.

I could keep wishing for something different.
Or I could do something different.

So, I **decided** to send an email.
One question. Less than 60 seconds.

And that one **action** changed how I showed up the next day.

That's how it works.

Notice. Decide. Act.

You don't outthink excuses. You interrupt them with action. And when you do, something changes inside you. You start redefining what progress really means.

REDEFINE PROGRESS

This book isn't about more effort. It's about more intention.

It's about preparing for the thoughts that will try to trap you and choosing to act quickly before they have a chance to stay.

It's about being honest with yourself, facing the mirror, and telling yourself the truth.

Every time you notice the Avoider, Blamer, Justifier, Doubter, or Pleaser showing up, decide what you can do about it, and then take immediate action.

Progress is about consistency. And it's about not quitting when you mess up.

It's 60 seconds of awareness. Followed by 60 seconds of action.

Change doesn't happen in hours. It happens in moments and minutes of each day. And it all begins with one simple truth.

You are only one choice away from living the life you want to live.

CHAPTER 3

The Friction Factor™

"Even if you're on the right track,
you'll get run over if you just sit there."
—Will Rogers

LET'S WORK BACKWARDS

At 17 years old, my biggest problem on the skeleton track in Park City, Utah, was corner 12.

Every time I drove my sled down the mountain, I slammed into the hard, icy wall.

Every. Single. Time.

The pain consumed me.

I obsessed over it. I braced for impact. And I feared what my body would look like at the bottom.

One night, after crawling off my sled at the finish line, my coach saw the pain on my face and asked a simple question.

"Where's the problem?"

I didn't hesitate.

"Corner 12," I said. *"I've literally tried everything. But the same thing keeps happening and it hurts so bad."*

He shoved his gloved hands into his pockets, looked up the track, and said,

"Well, when you're struggling in one spot, it usually starts somewhere else. So, let's work backwards."

So, we did.

Corner 11.
Problems.

Corner 10.
More problems.

We kept moving up the track until we reached corner 4.

That's where everything really fell apart.

"What are you doing in 4?" he asked.

I laughed. Then I fought back tears. I showed him my bleeding wrist and my torn speed suit. My left arm was covered in black, purple, and green bruises from constant impact with the walls.

I responded sarcastically.

"I'm crashing," I said. *"That's what I'm doing. I hit the wall in corner 4 and then ping-pong all the way down to 12 and that's where I slam the wall really hard. I don't think I can take another hit."*

He nodded. Calm. Unrattled. Like this wasn't new at all.

"There's the real problem," he said. *"Stop worrying about the rest of the track. Just focus on corner 4."*

I didn't want to hear that. I had already failed on this track more times than I could count and the idea of going back up the mountain felt unbearable.

Nothing about my situation felt fixable.

He must have seen the doubt and fear all over my face because he paused and said something that sounded like it came straight from Yoda.

*"Noelle, in this sport, it's not about **if** you crash. It's about **when** you do. What will you **choose** to do next? Athletes give up on themselves every day. Not because they aren't talented, but they quit when it gets hard. You've got to go back up the mountain, get back on your sled, and try*

again. It's part of the game we play. The friction will always be there. So, get used to it. What matters is what you choose to do with it."

I was speechless. His words were breathtaking.

Actually, I was in so much pain that I only caught every other word from that conversation. But luckily, he repeated it over the next few months until it really did change my perspective.

He knew that the pain in corner 12 wasn't the real problem. It started long before I crashed into the wall.

You know exactly what I'm talking about.

Maybe you keep crashing into the cupboard or the fast-food drive-thru while trying to lose weight.

Maybe you avoid the hard conversations in your marriage by staying busy. But the more you avoid the actual problems, the farther apart you drift in your relationship.

Or you dream of starting something new. A business. A book. A fresh chapter in life. But you tell yourself it's too late, too risky, or too unrealistic. So, you stay exactly where you don't want to be.

Where are you crashing?

What's something that you keep beating yourself up over because you keep failing to improve?

When you believe you're trapped, you stop trying because the friction feels unbearable.

The pain doesn't seem worth the effort.

And the moment you stop trying, excuses rush in to protect you.

If I could say your name right now, I would. And then I'd share the exact advice that my coach shared with me.

*"In this life, it's not about if you crash. With your goals. Your temper. Your ambition. But **when** you do, what will you **choose** to do next? You've got to quickly get back on track. It's part of life. The friction is real. Doughnuts. Freeway chaos. Health issues. Work projects. It will always be there. So just accept it. Ultimately, it's what you choose to do with the temptations*

and setbacks around you that will determine who you are and where you end up."

The conversation with my coach that night gave me just enough courage to go back up the mountain and try again.

Here's what experience teaches you.

The place where you feel the most pain is rarely where the real problem starts.

Corner 12 wasn't my issue.
Corner 4 was.

Once I stopped dreading corner 12 and started preparing for corner 4, everything changed.

I decided ahead of time how I would respond when the friction showed up. Before fear and panic could take over.

The wall didn't disappear. But my control improved. And with it, my energy, willpower, and confidence did too.

Day by day, the anxiety faded. One corner at a time. I fixed 5. Then 6. Then everything that came after.

15 years later, I stood at the top of the Park City track for the last time. I was competing for the United States on the World Cup circuit, and the 2014 Olympics were weeks away.

I pushed off.
I drove every line.
I was nearly flawless in corners 4 and 12.

When I crossed the finish line and looked up, I couldn't believe it.

I had shattered the track record and won World Cup gold.

Not because the friction disappeared. But because I finally learned where to manage it.

That conversation with my coach taught me something far bigger than how to handle a skeleton track.

It showed me that friction isn't the enemy.

Friction is the teacher.

Every crash, every setback, and every excuse reveals where you want to go and where you still need to grow.

Living with **NO EXCUSES** isn't about perfection. And it's not about trying harder.

It's about learning to work with friction instead of fighting it. It's about tracing the problem back to where it actually begins and taking decisive action from there.

That night, years ago, I discovered the foundation for what I call The Friction Factor™.

WHAT IS THE FRICTION FACTOR™?

For years, McDonald's believed the solution to declining performance was simple.

Just try harder.

They pushed more. Added options. And chased customers.

At first, that kind of friction worked. A little stretch can create growth. But McDonald's didn't stop there.

The menu kept growing.

Wraps. Salads. Specialty drinks.

On paper, it looked like expansion, but behind the counter, it felt very different.

Mistakes multiplied.
Employees burned out.
Customers waited longer.

By December 2014, it was clear they had crossed a line.

The problem wasn't effort. It was *too much friction.*

Too many decisions packed into every shift.
Too many steps between order and execution.

Too much resistance between what people wanted to do well and what the system allowed them to do.

And here's the part most people miss.

As friction increased, willpower drained faster than anyone expected.

Every added option required another decision.
Every added task pulled from the same limited energy reserve.

Eventually, even the most capable employees ran out of capacity.

That's when excuses show up.

Not because people don't care. But because they're depleted.

The friction that once helped them grow was now working against them. So, McDonald's did something that mattered.

They pulled back.
They simplified.
They cut menu items.

They streamlined processes and reduced the number of decisions employees had to make under pressure.

And almost immediately, the system moved back into balance.

Orders moved faster. Accuracy improved. Morale lifted and performance followed.

They didn't eliminate friction. They just brought it back to the center.

THE REAL REASON YOU FEEL STUCK

McDonald's didn't fail because people stopped trying. They failed because the friction got too high.

Friction is the resistance you feel when life pushes back. It shows up as pressure. Overwhelm. Exhaustion. It's that low-grade tension you carry all day without even realizing it. And when friction isn't managed, something predictable happens.

Excuses rush in.

Not because you're lazy. But because your brain is wired to protect you.

When friction rises beyond what your energy can support, your mind looks for relief and it offers explanations.

It whispers, *Not now. Try later. This isn't the right time.*

That's not weakness. That's being human. And once you understand this, the conversation changes.

You stop asking, *What's wrong with me?*

And start asking a far better question.

Where is friction out of balance?

THIS PATTERN SHOWS UP EVERYWHERE

Psychologists Robert Yerkes and John Dodson discovered something that still holds true today.

When we're not challenged enough, we get bored and lose motivation. When pressure becomes relentless, performance collapses under the weight of it.

But right in the middle, stress turns into fuel.

This is the science behind The Friction Factor™.

Excuses multiply at both extremes. And the sweet spot lives in the middle, where friction and willpower work together to create ownership, momentum, and growth.

When friction is balanced, it doesn't break you. It builds you. It teaches you.

As Seneca wrote, *"A gem cannot be polished without friction, nor a man perfected without trials."*

That's The Friction Factor™.

The Friction Factor™

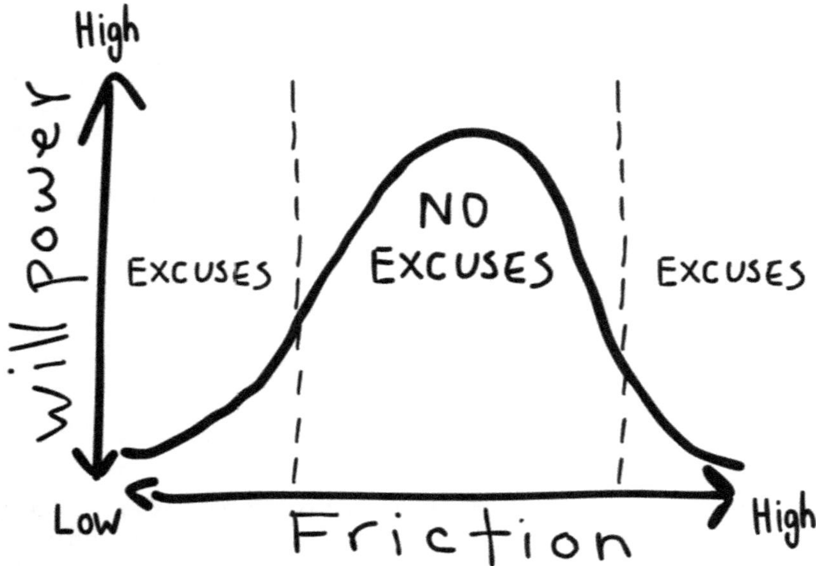

Too little friction and people disengage. Too much friction and people shut down.

But in the middle, where friction is centered and willpower is supported, excuses lose their power and a life of **NO EXCUSES** is found.

THE 2 PLACES PEOPLE GET STUCK

When willpower is high but friction is low, you land on the far left of the curve.

This is what you might call the space for "The Dreamer."

You want change, but nothing is pushing you out of your comfort zone. There's no urgency and no real demand to grow.

So, you wait.
You plan.
You hope.

Over time, too little friction breeds complacency and weakens confidence.

If this hits home for you, it may be time to push yourself. Set a new goal. Learn a new skill. Or challenge yourself in a new way.

At the other end of the curve, friction is too high. The pressure never lets up. Even the strongest willpower eventually runs out.

Burnout sets in.
Energy drains.
Excuses show up as relief.

If life feels overwhelming, it may be time to simplify. Set priorities. Declutter your schedule.

No matter where you are on the curve, alignment begins with awareness.

When you manage it well, friction becomes your ally and moves you into the **NO EXCUSES** zone in the middle.

TUNING THE TENSION

McDonald's didn't succeed by demanding more willpower or motivation from employees. They succeeded by tuning the tension in the system.

Think of it like tuning a guitar.

When the strings are too loose, there's no sound. When they're too tight, the strings snap. But when they're tuned just right, it creates harmony.

The same is true for you.

Too little friction and you grow comfortable. You drift. You stop stretching yourself.

Too much friction and you start to break. Your energy drains and burnout takes over.

When you learn to tune the tension with intention, friction stops fighting you and starts working for you.

WILLPOWER RUNS ON ENERGY

Alright. Now let's talk about willpower.

Think about that feeling on New Year's Day.

You wake up convinced *this* is the year.

Eat better. Work harder. Finally, stick to the plan.

You make a list so long it needs its own binder. Color-coded. Tabs included.

And for a few days, it works. Your willpower is really high.

But then life happens.

The days get long. Your energy drops. And suddenly the goals that once felt exciting start to feel really heavy.

And by January 9th, you've lost the binder.

You decide the problem must be you. Because if you wanted it bad enough, you should be able to stick with it, right?

So, you tell yourself you need more discipline. More grit. More motivation.

More willpower.

But here's the truth.

You're not failing.

You're just stuck at corner 12 and you don't know how to fix it.

You're exhausted with what's on your plate and what you really need is a better way to manage the energy that you have each day.

Because when energy drains, willpower fades and friction increases.

That's not weakness. That's biology.

If you want to reach your goals, stop beating yourself up and start working backward. Look at your corner 4. Look at where your energy goes before things fall apart. Because this is actually an energy problem.

Willpower runs on energy. And when energy falls, if you're not prepared for it, your choices will suffer.

Here's the thing. You don't have unlimited willpower.

Psychologists call this ego depletion.

All it really means is that self-control runs out over time. You get tired as the hours pass. And then even the smallest choices can feel harder than they need to be.

Let's come back to The Friction Factor™ graph so we can see what this looks like.

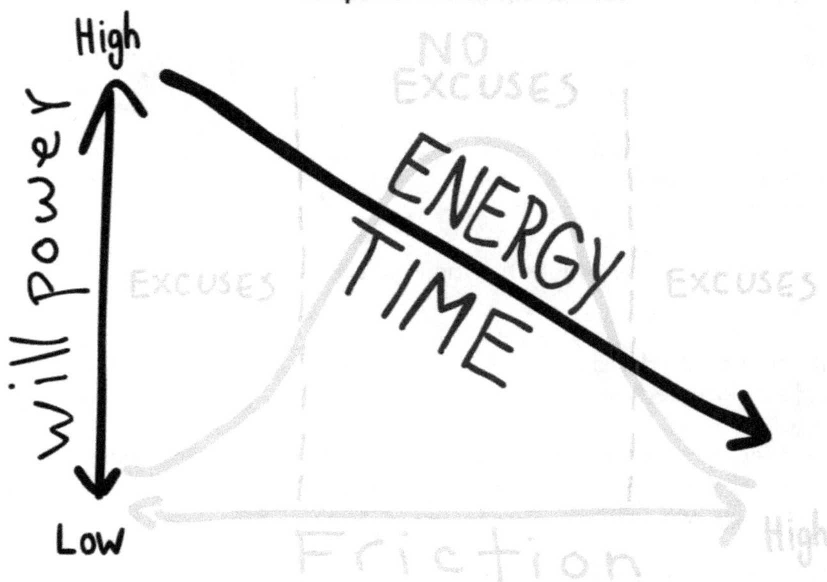

Every decision you make, every temptation you resist and every emotion you manage costs energy. As the day goes on, that reserve shrinks. And when energy drops, good choices get harder.

That's why you eat healthy in the morning and give up at night.
Why you're patient at work and short at home.
Why you start the week strong and feel off by Thursday.

Excuses fill in the gaps and run your day.

It's not because you stopped caring. It's that you got tired.

Trying harder isn't the answer. Managing your energy is.

BURNOUT IS A FRICTION PROBLEM

Look at the healthcare industry.

Physicians are some of the most disciplined, capable, and committed professionals in the world. They spend years training to do work that truly matters.

And yet, burnout is everywhere.

The American Medical Association reported that nearly 50% of physicians in the United States show symptoms of burnout.

Not because they lack purpose.
Not because they stopped caring.
Not because they aren't capable.

They're exhausted because the friction never stops.

Long hours.
Life-and-death decisions.
Endless documentation.

For every hour spent with a patient, nearly 2 more are spent clicking boxes, writing notes, and managing systems that were never designed to support human energy.

That kind of friction doesn't make people stronger. It makes them crash at corner 12.

EXCUSES ARE A SIGNAL

Here's the bottom line.

2 things open the door to excuses.

Fear.
And comfort.

Fear shows up in friction. Comfort shows up when willpower runs out.

When friction is too low or too high, excuses show up.

And when energy isn't protected, your willpower suffers and your brain looks for relief. Not progress.

That's when excuses start to sound reasonable.

"I'll start tomorrow."
"I just don't have it today."
"Once things slow down."

Those aren't lies. They're signals.

Signals that energy has dropped below what the friction requires.

Living with **NO EXCUSES** doesn't mean pushing harder through exhaustion. It means learning when to push and when to pause.

Physicians don't need more motivation. They need to start at corner 4.

Better systems.
Clearer priorities.
Protected energy.

So do you.

Because when energy is restored, willpower returns. And when willpower and friction are aligned, progress feels sustainable.

STOP SKIPPING THE HARD PART

THE PROBLEM THAT SHOWS UP ON SCHEDULE

I love sitting around the table with my family. I just hate deciding what's for dinner.

5 o'clock shows up every single day, and somehow, I'm still surprised by it.

The kids ask, *"What's for dinner?"*

And immediately, my stress spikes. My patience thins. And I think, *didn't we just do this yesterday?*

That moment feels ike a major crash.

It's a wall in my day. It's my corner 12.

I'm tired. Decisions feel heavy. And I somehow convince my family that cereal has all the food groups necessary to sustain life.

But the problem didn't actually start at 5 P.M. It started the day before, when I skipped the grocery store and told myself I didn't have time.

That was my corner 4.

So, I've made a small change.

Every Sunday, I now take a minute to find 5 simple dinner recipes for the week and add them to my shopping list.

That's it.

I make it a consistent part of my week. And now, when 5 P.M. comes on the weekdays, the friction eases because I have a plan.

Same family hunger.
Same time of day.
Very different experience.

FRICTION ISN'T RANDOM

If you want to manage friction, you have to stop being surprised by it.

Pericles, one of ancient Greece's greatest leaders, put it simply.

"Time is the wisest counselor of all."

Time doesn't just pass. It teaches. And when you pay attention to it, patterns show up in your energy and your willpower.

The same stress.
The same excuses.
The same moments that derail you.

Not because you're failing but because you're human.

And once you start listening to time, friction stops ambushing you and it begins to guide you.

So, let's name the wall and work backward from there.

FIND YOUR CORNER 4

CORNER 12: NAME THE WALL

There's a place in your life where you keep promising yourself it will be different next time.

You reset. You re-commit. You tell yourself you're serious now. And then, somehow, you end up right back where you started.

For most people, this shows up in everyday life.

The morning routine you can't stick with. The cold calls you keep delaying. The neighbor you keep avoiding.

That's your corner 12.

It feels like the problem because it's where the frustration shows up. It's loud. It hurts and it demands your attention.

Just like skeleton athletes sliding down a track, most people have more than one corner where crashes happen. But just pick one.

One area of life you want to improve.

Your health. Your job. A relationship.

Say it out loud.
Write it down.

And be honest with yourself. Because corner 12 isn't failure. It's feedback and it's trying to teach you something.

CORNER 4: LOOK EARLIER

Now here's where most people get stuck.

They try harder at the wall.

I see this constantly with professionals who care deeply about their work.

A salesperson misses quota and pushes longer hours. A manager feels behind and adds more meetings. A healthcare worker runs on fumes and tells themselves to tough it out.

More effort. More pressure. Less margin. More crashes.

But corner 12 didn't start there.

So, pause and work backward.

Ask yourself where things begin to slip *before* the crash.

In your health, corner 4 might be the late nights you keep justifying. The workouts you stopped prioritizing. The recovery you never protect.

At work, it might be the meetings you didn't need to accept. The projects you don't know how to start. The lack of growth that quietly drained your motivation.

In relationships, it's often the conversation you keep postponing. The resentment you don't name. The time you stopped investing.

Write it down. Don't skip this part.

When you write it down, it becomes an accountability partner between you and yourself.

This isn't about blame. It's about awareness.

That quiet drain you've been overlooking, that's your corner 4.

THE 60 SECONDS SHIFT

Now here's the good news.

Change doesn't require a dramatic reset. It requires one intentional adjustment earlier on the track.

That's your 60 seconds shift.

Maybe it's setting a firm bedtime. 10 o'clock hits and the screens go off. You slow your brain down. You protect your sleep so tomorrow's energy doesn't start depleted.

Maybe it's clarifying your top priority in the morning before the noise takes over.

Or perhaps it's finally calling the doctor, pulling out your running shoes, or closing the 27 tabs that have been open for months so your brain can focus on one thing at a time.

The goal isn't to eliminate all the friction in your life. The goal is to recognize it and then manage it.

When you prepare differently at corner 4, corner 12 starts to change on its own. The wall doesn't disappear. But you stop slamming into it and you cross the finish line with energy to spare.

USE FRICTION TO YOUR ADVANTAGE

THE LESSON I DIDN'T EXPECT

On the flight to the 2014 Olympic Games in Russia, my 6-year-old daughter, Lacee, stared out the window as the plane pushed back from the gate.

She watched quietly for a moment, then said,

"That's funny. We have to move backward before we can go forward."

I smiled.

And then it hit me.

She was right.

Sometimes progress looks like retreat. Sometimes forward motion starts with a pause.

That single sentence pulled me straight back to a cold night on the track and a question my coach asked years earlier when I slammed into corner 12.

"Where's the problem? Let's work backwards."

THE PROBLEM ISN'T THE PROBLEM

In life and leadership, the problem we feel isn't always the problem we need to fix.

A doctor may believe patients aren't listening when the real problem is an overscheduled calendar that leaves no time for meaningful conversations.

A CFO may feel constant tension around budget limits when the deeper issue is a CEO unwilling to listen to financial insight.

Or a company may blame employees for mistakes when the real friction lives upstream in unclear expectations or flawed systems.

The symptom gets all the attention. The source gets ignored. And we keep crashing into the same wall.

COSTCO LOOKED AT THE REAL PROBLEM

During the Great Recession, around 2009, when most retailers were cutting wages to survive, Costco made a decision that confused Wall Street. Instead of trimming labor costs, they raised pay.

Leadership stepped back and questioned the assumption everyone else accepted.

What if the real problem wasn't wages but exhaustion, turnover, and disengagement?

By investing more in their people, Costco reduced friction throughout the system.

Employees stayed longer. Productivity increased and customers felt the difference.

By going backward on what looked like the obvious fix, Costco moved forward in every way that mattered.

PAUSE. LISTEN. ADJUST.

We usually spend more time and energy working around problems than trying to solve them.

Think about that guitar that's out of tune.

You wouldn't strum harder and hope for better sound.

You'd stop.
Listen.
Make a small adjustment.

And even then, you'd expect to tune it again. Because temperature changes. Time passes and strings loosen.

Life works the same way.

Living with **NO EXCUSES** doesn't mean forcing your way through friction. It means pausing long enough to make the right adjustment. Again, and again.

It's a rhythm.

Notice.
Adjust.
Move forward.

Find your corner 4's and start improving them one small step at a time.

You're not looking for a dramatic overhaul. You're looking for progress you can sustain.

Small wins matter. Microscopic improvements count. Reasonable expectations keep you moving instead of quitting.

When friction is managed with intention, energy begins to return. And when energy is stronger, willpower doesn't have to fight so hard.

It shows up ready for the day and that's when excuses lose their leverage. Not because motivation suddenly appeared, but because the path feels doable.

And here's the reassuring part.

Friction is part of life.

It always has been. It always will be.

The difference now is that you know how to work with it.

The friction you feel isn't random. It's a signal pointing toward improvement.

Living with **NO EXCUSES** doesn't mean it's friction free. It means you know how to use the friction to your advantage. One corner at a time.

CHAPTER 4

Own Your Progress

"Take ownership. Don't make excuses.
Don't blame any other person or anything else."
—*Jocko Willink*

WHERE YOU LOOK IS WHERE YOU GO

The most difficult track in the world sits on the eastern border of Germany, just a few miles from the Czech Republic.

It was my first time competing in Europe, and as the youngest athlete on the World Cup team, I carried that silent, heavy pressure to impress everyone.

We touched down in Munich. Piled into vans. And drove 5 hours to the dreaded track.

I was in the corner of the athlete's room trying to build up my confidence when the team decided to join in with their own "pep talk."

If you want to call it that.

So, picture this.

I'm minding my own business, getting my head in the game, when my teammate, Chris strolls up to me and says,

"Hey. Just so you know. This is the most dangerous track in the world."

Oh GREAT.

That's exactly what you want to hear just moments before you launch yourself down an ice chute at 90 miles an hour.

Then, with a smile on his face, he keeps going.

"Be ready for curve 4. If you miss your steer by an inch, you'll hit the roof and crash."

Awesome.

Love that for me.

Before I can even roll my eyes, another teammate jumps in.

"Curve 4? No. Curve 9 is the killer. Miss that one and you're toast."

Fantastic. Truly uplifting.

Then, because apparently this is a group activity now, another teammate chimes in.

"Forget those. Curve 10 and 12 will tear you to pieces. But honestly? I doubt you'll even make it that far."

Wow.

Peak moral support right there. Really feeling the love.

But here's the truth.

I had already stopped listening. Completely tuned them out. Because the second they started listing all the ways this track could chew me up and spit me out, my brain took over, and I spiraled down a tunnel of doom and gloom.

I *should* have been confident.

I had elite coaches.
Solid equipment.
Hours of track footage.

And hello! I was competing on the World Cup circuit.

But this is where I missed it.

Making the team felt like the finish line. In reality, it was just the starting point and I hadn't prepared for it.

I simply told myself to suck it up. I didn't think I could learn any more than I already knew. So, I slapped on my tough face and pretended I wasn't terrified.

Once my teammates walked away from the motivational meeting, I immediately strapped volleyball knee pads on my elbows and shoved pieces of a foam camping mattress under my speed suit. It was my high-tech effort to protect myself from whatever this track was about to do to me.

I no longer cared to impress anyone. I was in sheer survival mode.

A veteran athlete from Japan was called to the line. She placed her sled on the ice, sprinted down the chute, jumped on, and disappeared into curve one.

Her 60 seconds on the track had begun.

I watched the clock and felt the pressure build.

Tick. Tock. Tick. Tock.

27 seconds. 28. 29.

Then, it stopped ticking.

Halfway through her run, the announcer's voice cut through the speakers.

"Achtung! Achtung! 81 im die bahn!"

I learned quickly that he had shouted, *"Attention! Attention! 81 in the track!"*

81 meant she crashed. She was off her sled and needed medical assistance.

Paramedics rushed in. Loaded her into a van and carried her away to the hospital.

Right then Chris ran up to me, with a much more serious expression than before and said,

"Noelle! I forgot to tell you! No matter what you do, do NOT get in the krankenwagen! They don't have doctors in this town. They take you to the vet! They treat you next to the horses and cows and pigs! And we don't know when we'd be able to see you again!"

I was speechless. But my eyebrows said, *"You've got to be kidding me."*

By the way, *krankenwagen* means ambulance in German. Not exactly the first foreign word you expect to learn. But it was mine.

I took a deep breath and tried to calm myself, but my mind had other plans.

Curve 4. Okay I got this.
Curve 9, 10, 12, 15, 21.
Wait. Aren't there only 19 curves on this track?
Maybe I shouldn't go today. No, Noelle, you can do this. You are a world-class athlete. Right? Right? Holy crap. What am I even doing here?

It was a full-on internal meltdown and I was the only one who could hear it.

The green light came on.

I had 30 seconds to move.

So, I adjusted my weak sauce volleyball pads, set my sled down, and inched forward. One slow step in front of the other.

Buying time. Delaying the inevitable.

Once I passed the crest, there was no turning back. I dropped onto my sled and tried to steer through the fear.

Curve 1. Curve 2.

A tiny flicker of hope. *Okay, I can do this.*

Then I slammed the wall out of curve 3, shot to the roof in curve 4, and flipped onto my back.

"Nope. I can't do this!"

But the next curve turned the opposite direction and rolled me back onto my runners.

So, I yelled out loud,

"YES! I'm so good at this sport!"

My voice echoed down the track.

I barely had time to celebrate when curve 9 came out of nowhere and launched me onto my back. Again.

All I could think was,

"This is it. I'm actually going to die."

I slid down the straight-away on my back. Gripping my sled for dear life.

Pause for a second here because there's something you've got to understand.

Before this trip down the ice, I had **never** flipped on my back. Not once. I wasn't even halfway down this track and I had already been on my back **twice!** I was in pure panic mode.

Alright, back to the story.

Somehow, I flipped myself back onto my sled just before the next corner.

Curve 10. *"Kreisel."* A full 360-degree turn.

The biggest curve in the world.

The second I entered the corner, the pressure suctioned my body to the ice like super glue locked between your fingers.

I couldn't move a muscle.

My mind went blank. I didn't know what to do. So, I did the only thing I could.

I held on.

My sled found its own rhythm. Rising toward the roof, dropping back down, then rising again.

I could feel the speed. The vibrations. The force.

And I had zero control.

I was terrified.

The world was flying by at a million miles an hour and there was nothing that I could do about it.

I knew the exit of the curve was coming. So, with every ounce of strength I had, I lifted my head against the G-forces to see what was in front of me.

That's when I saw it.

I was flying straight up toward the scarred wooden roof. Inching closer and closer to that piece of wood that's meant to keep a sled from flying out of the track.

I anticipated the pcin it was about to cause and I couldn't take my eyes off of it.

One thought flashed through my mind.

"Don't hit the wood. Please don't hit the wood."

Time slowed right before impact.

BAM!

A bolt of pain tore through the left side of my body, and suddenly I was airborne.

White ice. Pine trees. Sky.

Everything flickered past as I slammed onto the frozen track 10 feet below. My 65-pound sled crashed onto my chest and knocked the air out of me.

I couldn't breathe.

Panic surged through every cell in my body.

I pushed the sled away and felt the ice shredding through my speed suit as I slid through the next curves on my back.

I rolled to my stomach and pushed up. Fire ripped through my hands and knees as I fought to slow down.

When I finally came to a stop, my lungs felt like they were sucking air through a straw.

Pain shot through my arm, and blood dripped through my speed suit.

My "high-tech" padding obviously failed me. It was scattered all over the track behind me.

A yard sale of foam and volleyball gear.

Then, in the distance, I saw them coming. The paramedics. Running toward me. In slow motion.

When they reached me, all I could say was, *"Nein krankenwagon."*

That was the extent of my German.

No ambulance.

I insisted I was fine, so eventually they let me go.

But here's the part that changed everything for me.

Beyond the lesson about not getting into a vet ambulance in a small German town, I learned something bigger that day. Something I've carried with me ever since.

That day on the track, my goal was to cross the finish line. That was the plan. And I had every resource to help me get there.

I had coaches.
I had equipment.
I had knowledge at my fingertips.

But I was overwhelmed by the track. And somehow, I had convinced myself that putting in a minimal effort would be enough.

I decided not to take any extra time to learn or study. And I was unprepared.

This caused me to focus on my fear. My doubts. My anxiety and all the skills I didn't have when I really needed them most.

And I crashed. Hard.

Something as small and simple as shifting my eyes to where I wanted to go, rather than where I didn't want to end up, would have allowed me to steer my sled to the finish line.

It would have changed everything.

That day, I learned this priceless lesson.

I learned that **where you look is where you go.**

That's the truth beyond the ice.

The problem isn't the track. It's not the pressure. It's not the industry, no matter how difficult it is or how quickly it moves.

Those are just excuses.

I kept staring at the roof.
I focused on my stress. My pain points. And everything I didn't know.
And I hit it spot on.

So, ask yourself this.

Where are you looking today?

Are you focused on your stress? Your fears? Your anxiety?
Are you focused on the skills you don't have or how far behind you feel?
Or are your sights set on where you want to go and how you'll get there?
Are you taking ownership of your learning in a world that moves faster every single day?

Because in tech, AI, and any fast-paced industry, things change in seconds.

You want to succeed?
Then own it.

You want to be prepared for that promotion?
Stop staring at the roof.

Success follows the people who take responsibility for their own progress.

Study the skills that matter. Experiment with new tools. Learn from the people who are already doing it well and pay attention to how they operate.

Make learning non-negotiable so you stay ready for what comes next. Your future depends on what you choose to focus on.

And never ever forget this.

Where you look is where you go.

OWN YOUR GROWTH

Learning cultures win. Period.

This isn't just a nice idea. We can see it in the data.

LinkedIn's Workplace Learning Report found that companies with a strong learning culture don't just grow. They thrive.

They see 57% higher retention, 23% more internal moves, and 7% more promotions into management roles than organizations that treat learning as an afterthought.

That's huge for industries trying to retain top-tier employees.

In a world where talent can leave with one click, learning is your competitive edge.

3 QUESTIONS. 60 SECONDS. MASSIVE GROWTH.

Netflix is one of the most influential companies in the world. And at the center is cofounder Reed Hastings.

He said, *"You have to focus on one thing where you're clear on what kind of impact you want to have. Otherwise, you never get anything done."*

That day on the track, I learned the same lesson the hard way. I was focused on everything at once and it overwhelmed me. What I really needed was to focus on improving one thing at a time.

I knew that no one was going to steer the sled for me.
No one was going to make me better.

If I wanted to improve, I had to own it.

That meant studying.
Preparing.
And getting very specific about what needed to change.

So, I created a new habit. A small one. An easy one.

I began asking myself these 3 simple questions every night before bed.

I call it **The Daily 3.**

1. **What went well today?**
2. **What didn't go so well?**
3. **How will I choose to improve tomorrow?**

That's it.

This habit takes about 60 seconds. And it launched me to success.

Massive success.

Less than a year later, I was ranked first in the world. Not because I overhauled my life. But because I chose to improve one small thing every single day.

Try this.

Ask yourself these 3 questions.

THE DAILY 3

Question 1: *What went well today?*

Really think about it.

We're so wired to rush past our wins that we forget to notice them. But you did something today.

You showed up.

Maybe you finished a project.
Maybe you took the very first step toward healing or recovery.
Or you learned one thing that will save you a little time in the future.

Give yourself credit for what went well.

Question 2: *What didn't go so well today?*

Be honest. Be vulnerable.

Maybe you lost your temper or failed your diet... again.
Maybe you're falling behind on a project because you don't know the next step. Or you're clinging to outdated tools or old software because learning the new platform feels overwhelming.

Whatever it is, own it.

Once you own it, you can learn from it.

Question 3: *How will I choose to improve tomorrow?*

This is where growth actually happens.

Not in the goals you write down once a year. But in the minutes you choose to get a little better.

Listen to a podcast on your commute that improves your skills.
Explore a new AI tool for 5 minutes.
Decide before you even start the car that you're going to be a patient driver.

Keep it simple. Keep it specific.

The Daily 3 is where medals are won.

This is how promotions are earned. This is how consistency happens. This is how organizations rise.

GET YOURSELF UP

When I was 6 years old and learning to snow ski, I discovered something surprisingly profound.

I had one of those dramatic kid crashes.

Skis went flying in opposite directions.
Poles vanished completely.

And I ended up flat on my back, staring up at the sky like a game of pickup sticks gone wrong.

I just stayed there. Watching snowflakes land on my face.

Waiting for someone to notice I was missing.

My dad had skied ahead, and I'm sure he was close. But at that moment it felt like I had been abandoned on the mountain.

After what was probably 30 seconds but seemed like forever, the truth hit me.

"No one's coming. If I don't move from this spot, I'll be stuck here forever. Come on, Noelle. You've got to get yourself up."

Upskilling works the same way.

No one learns for you. Even on a team, you own your growth. You stand up, do the work, and get yourself down the mountain.

A recent McKinsey survey of tech-focused organizations found that 80% of leaders agree that the fastest way to close skill gaps isn't in waiting things out.

It's upskilling.

Not waiting for the market to calm down.
Not hoping talent magically appears.

But choosing to grow the people you already have.

On purpose.
Every day.

That's the path forward. And it's available to anyone willing to learn.

DON'T WAIT. INNOVATE.

Heading into the 2010 Winter Olympic Games, I kept running into problems with my sled.

One malfunction after another. One broken part stacked on top of the next.

Most athletes and coaches shrugged and said it was part of the sport. You fix what breaks, you lose time, and you move on.

But my husband, Janson, refused to accept that.

He saw the frustration and lost time and decided he wasn't going to stand by and let equipment dictate performance.

So, he did something every smart company would immediately recognize as a hire-worthy skill.

He took initiative. He innovated. He stepped in to improve the system.

Without being asked by anyone, Janson opened the skeleton specification rule book.

Nearly a thousand pages of tiny print and technical details that would thrill an aerospace engineer.

He read every line.

Then he got to work.

Day after day, he designed. He identified what needed to be fixed. He learned where the regulations allowed for creativity.

He built my sled for the 2010 Olympic Games and another for 2014 with new improvements.

And here's the extraordinary part.

He's not an engineer. He doesn't have the certifications people assume you need.

What he has is drive. Curiosity. Hunger.

A willingness to learn everything he can and the initiative to put that learning into action.

Many nations pour millions of dollars into research and development to build the fastest, most aerodynamic sleds in the world.

And he surpassed them. Again, and again.

That's what happens when someone chooses to grow without waiting for permission.

Janson believed something massive was possible, so he went for it. And the moment he gave himself permission to dream big, everything else expanded.

He showed up with more purpose at work. More confidence in the community. More intention in life.

The moment you expand what you believe is possible in one area of your life, everything else expands with it.

You take more risks.
You learn faster.
And you say yes to new skills because you can finally see a future worth growing toward.

STANDING AT THE EDGE OF WHAT'S NEXT

In the months leading up to the Olympics in Sochi, Russia, in 2014, I knew it would be my final race. And I felt something I never expected.

Emptiness.

For 15 years I'd lived with absolute clarity. Every decision, every sacrifice, every early morning was driven by one goal.

Compete in the Olympics.

But as the Games approached, I realized that once they ended, I would retire, and I would be staring at a blank slate.

No plan. No next step. And that terrified me.

You know exactly what this feels like.

When the job ends, the season ends, the role ends, and you realize how much of your identity was tied to it.

John C. Maxwell said growth is the only guarantee that tomorrow gets better. And he's exactly right.

Just days before the opening ceremonies, I knew I needed to keep moving forward.

Keep growing. Learning. Becoming.

So, Janson and I decided to do something about it. We sat down in our rental house in Russia and created a list of what it would look like to live with no regrets.

I wrote down things I had always wanted to try, learn, see, do, and be.

I wanted to learn guitar, memorize constellations, write a book, speak on stages, and even juggle.

Our No Regrets List is still growing today and it's been absolutely liberating.

We've golfed in Scotland. Learned Spanish in Costa Rica. Earned an MBA.

And I wrote this book!

I've even learned to beatbox a pattern here and there.

We've done all this by deciding not to wait.

I call it **The No Regrets List**.

It's not complicated. Just 3 steps.

This list helps you dream boldly, choose what matters most, and take action so you never look back wishing you'd done more.

That's what I want for you now. So, grab something to write on.

I love using a big piece of butcher paper and colorful markers. But you can use anything.

No limits. **NO EXCUSES.**

THE NO REGRETS LIST

STEP 1: Write Your 20

Alright. Here's what you're going to do. For the next few minutes, give yourself permission to dream.

You're going to write down anything you want to see, be, have, learn, know, or do.

Anything.

This is your No Regrets List, so don't hold back and don't overthink it.

If you were at the end of your life looking back and you had no regrets, what would you have seen, learned, or become?

Write it down. Make it messy.

Maybe you want to ride a horse at sunset or shake hands with your favorite author. Or maybe you want to build an app that solves a real problem.

Here are a few more ideas:

Swim in every ocean.
Paint with Bob Ross.
Learn an instrument.
Learn a language.
Start a podcast.
Take your dream trip.
Learn how to sew.
Join a civic outreach program.
Write a book.

It doesn't matter how big or small it sounds. If it lights something up inside you, write it down.

But here's the thing. You *must* write at *least* 20 things.

That's the rule. 20 possibilities.

Fill the page.

STEP 2: Underline Your Top 3

Do you feel that?

It's waking something up in you. It's reconnecting you to possibility. It's reminding you that you're allowed to want things and that you are allowed to grow.

Once you have your 20, take a minute to underline your top 3.

Which ones scare you in the best way?
Which ones make your heart beat a little faster?
Which ones make you think, "Oh... that would be incredible"?

Those 3.

Put a line under them.

STEP 3: Circle 1 and Get to Work

Now choose one.

Just one.

Circle it. And circle it again.

That's your new beginning.
That's the thing you're no longer making excuses about.

Tell someone about it. Break it down into small steps. And get to work.

You don't have to do everything. You just have to start with one dream and one bold choice to move.

Remember that day on the ski hill? No one lifted me out of the snow. I had to do it myself. And now it's your turn.

Push your excuses aside and take action.

Living with **NO EXCUSES** means living the no regrets life.

SMALL CHOICES, BIG RESULTS

YOUR REAL COMPETITION ISN'T OTHER PEOPLE

Over the years, after competing on the world stage and staring down more fear than I ever admitted out loud, I learned something that shocked me.

I was never actually competing against anyone else.

It blew me away when I realized this.

No matter what's happening in your life, you're not actually competing against anyone else.

Not the people in your industry. Not the coworkers who seem a step ahead. Not the companies with bigger budgets or flashier tools.

Your real competition is happening inside you.

It's your procrastination and the tiny delays that sabotage your momentum.
It's your ego, convincing you that you don't need to prepare for a deadline. And the unhealthy choices you keep making when no one is watching.

Your real opponent is the distraction you call "just checking." The bad habits you repeat on autopilot and the skill you keep putting off learning because it feels uncomfortable.

Once you finally get honest with yourself, something powerful happens.

The people around you stop feeling like opponents, and you start realizing you've had the power the whole time.

Because your biggest breakthroughs won't come from outrunning someone else. They'll come from closing the gap between who you are and who you want to be.

And when you make a clear plan for yourself each day, you eliminate the opponents that are keeping you stuck

THE FIRST CHOICE OF YOUR DAY

Almost everyone has this backward.

They think their first choice of the day happens at sunrise.

Wrong.

It happens at 9 p.m. the night before.

That's the moment your morning actually begins. It's the moment you decide to make a plan for the next day.

This is where you use **The Daily 3.**

When you climb into bed tonight, ask yourself the 3 questions:

1. **What went well?**
2. **What didn't go so well?**
3. **How will I choose to improve tomorrow?**

Write your answers down.

When your alarm goes off in the morning, you already know the kind of day you want to have and exactly who you want to become.

No questions. No delay. Self-discipline is on your side.

WIN THE FIRST MINUTE

Your morning is the launch sequence of your entire day. The first choice you make when the alarm goes off sets the rhythm for every choice that follows.

Robin Sharma said it best in his book, *The 5 AM Club.*

"Own your morning. Elevate your life."

He's spot on.

When you wake up, own your morning.

Sit up. Take one deep breath. Move your body, even for 60 seconds.

Then, visualize the thing you're improving today. Because your morning is your momentum for the day.

OWN YOUR LEARNING

It all circles back to what I learned from hitting that wooden roof of the track in 2003.

Where you look is where you go.

Look at the opportunities around you. Upskill. Learn more. Be humble. Take advantage of the tools at your fingertips.

You change your life the second you decide to focus on where you want to go rather than where you don't want to end up.

Whether it's after they finish a golf match or a track meet or as they're walking out the door to school, I often tell my kids this.

"You win some, you learn some. You only lose some if you never learn."

Owning your progress isn't about talent, timing, or luck. It's about choosing to learn and grow in every way possible. And when you choose to learn each day, no one and nothing can stop you.

CHAPTER 5

The Power of the Next 60 Seconds

"You are one decision away from a completely different life."
—*Mel Robbins*

THE ONLY MINUTE THAT COUNTS

It all came down to the next 60 seconds.

It always does.

There were countless minutes that could have derailed this moment. But here I was, standing at the starting line. Facing another minute that really mattered.

This was my fourth and final run at the 2007 World Championship skeleton race in St. Moritz, Switzerland. And everything felt still.

The track. The air. Even my thoughts slowed.

Most races are powered by routine.
You warm up. You follow the process. You trust the muscle memory and go.

But this race was different. This one asked more of me.
Physically. Mentally. Emotionally.

I stared down the track, waiting for the green light.

The starting line in St. Moritz is different. When you stand there and look down the track, you know one thing for sure.

You're not finishing where you started.

In St. Moritz, you launch in one town and you finish in another town entirely.
The town of Celerina.

This is where bobsled, luge, and skeleton were born back in the 1800s, and the traditions here are deep.

For example, every other track in the world counts the corners.

Corner 1.
Corner 2.
Corner 3.

Nice and orderly, right?

But not here.

Here, every corner has a name. And a reputation.

Tree.
Wall.
Horseshoe.

They sound friendly but they're not. You hit one, bounce off another, and get flung through the third.

And if your kids are anything like mine, then you've watched *Frozen* a hundred times and probably wondered,

"Why is everyone cutting ice out of a lake?"

Well, this is why.

For generations, people here have continued to cut blocks of ice straight from Lake St. Moritz and build this track by hand each year.

One frozen block at a time. It's truly spectacular.

I knew I was standing at the starting line that day because of the choices that led me there. So many choices.

Small ones. Hard ones. Repeated ones.

And a lot of moments where I almost talked myself out of continuing.

As I waited for the athlete before me to finish her final run of this competition, I glanced down at my right leg and smiled.

I had come SO far in the past year. That alone felt like a win.

And that's when my brain decided to get involved.

You know this moment.

Everything gets quiet. And suddenly your brain says, *"Great. Let's talk about why you're really here."*

So, my mind went back to last season.

One year earlier, the Olympics were in Torino, Italy. I was ranked first in the world rankings and the gold jersey had my name on it. But I never even got the chance to wear it. Earlier that season, during a practice run at our Olympic Trials, I was hit by a 1,400-pound, 4-man bobsled. My right leg shattered. And just like that, my Olympic dream ended.

There was no closure. The team moved on. And I was left behind. Just an ambulance ride. Surgery. And rehab.

As my bones began to heal, the excuses showed up fast. And they made sense too.

You're injured. You'll never be the same. Just quit.

And honestly, quitting would have been easy.

But here's what I learned.

Excuses don't lose power when life gets easier. They lose power when you choose to take action even when quitting feels reasonable.

2 weeks after the accident, I got back on my sled just to see if I could still slide. I knew no one would approve of it. Not the doctors. Not my coaches. But I had to try.

So, I put on a wig and used a fake name. I couldn't even stand, so I begged my husband, Janson, to push me down the mountain.

That's one way to test your marriage.

He held onto my sled handle, sprinted from the starting line and pushed me into corner 1. Crutches were waiting at the bottom of the track so I could hobble away.

NO EXCUSES are what you choose when the dream still matters to you.

Filmmaker, Matthew Fultz documented my entire effort to comeback from the bobsled accident and titled it "114 Days: The Race to Save a Dream."

The film captured the hope of recovery. The challenges. The heartache. All of it.

3 weeks after wearing the wig, I was in Europe competing on the World Cup circuit. But despite my miraculous comeback, I barely missed out on making the Olympic team. And that's how the documentary ends. With raw and honest emotions that come from a broken heart.

Instead of competing in the Games, I had to watch the 2006 Olympic race from a television screen.

It turns out watching your dream unfold feels very different when someone sitting next to you asks if you want popcorn.

After missing the Olympics, excuses hit me hard. And they came from every direction.

I wanted to blame. I wanted to justify. And I wanted to avoid people and conversations altogether.

The truth is, I wanted to shut down.

I told myself I was fine. I told everyone I was fine. And then I did what driven people often do when their identity gets shaken.

I stayed busy.

Less than a month after the season ended, I enrolled in an MBA program. Because there's nothing like a graduate degree to make avoidance feel productive. Going back to school felt like progress. And it was respectable. But honestly, it was an exit strategy.

I didn't think I'd ever come back to compete, and I needed something to move toward.

A few months went by and somehow my husband Janson talked me into going back to compete. He said something like,

"You've gotta get back on the horse or you might regret it."

First of all, what horse?
And second. I knew he was right.

I had come so close to becoming an Olympian and if I didn't go back right then, it would be over forever.

So, I agreed.
Hesitantly.

And the instant I did, the doubts showed up in unexpected ways.

You don't even know where to start.
You're already so far behind.
You should wait until you're ready.

You've been here too.

That moment when you convince yourself you need a full plan, with zero risk and maximum comfort, before starting. When all you really need is one small move.

Excuses always show up that way. As subtle thoughts and partial truths. And every time one entered my mind, I knew I had a choice to make.

Believe it or question it.

One day, the excuses were particularly loud. So, I decided to do something about it.

I pulled my sled out of the garage and put it in our living room. It basically became a centerpiece in our home. I knew I wouldn't be able to walk past it without remembering the decision I had made to compete again.

That was all I did that day.
One minute. One action.
And it was enough.

Seeing that sled every day reminded me that action silences doubt.

When I began working out again, commitment looked like one rep. One set. Training alone in a basement. No applause and no guarantees.

Doubt and fear were constant rivals during recovery. Some days I won. And some days they absolutely did. But I noticed something.

Every time an excuse showed up, there was a window. A small one. If I accepted the excuse, I stayed stuck. If I questioned it and moved anyway, something shifted inside of me.

And this is what I realized.
I could control what I did in the next 60 seconds.
And honestly, that's the only minute that counts.

It was finally time to race.

This was my final run at the World Championships. The gold medalist from the Olympics the previous year was sitting in the leader's box. This was her home track and she knew it well.

The green light flashed, signaling it was my turn to go.

I pushed off the block, sprinted, and dove headfirst onto my sled. The clock was ticking.

I could feel the speed immediately and the force through each curve was heavy.

I steered through the corners with precision. I drove the sled meticulously using the pressure from my shoulders and knees.

The timing mattered.

Everything matters when you are moving at freeway speeds and pulling 5 G's. My breath. My vision. My focus. And on this track, even blinking at the wrong time will cost you greatly.

I was committed to every movement.

The track was blazing fast. Faster than anything I'd ever experienced.

The clock stopped as I slid across the finish line. Relief hit first. Then certainty. I knew I had used my 60 seconds well. Not just on the track, but in the countless decisions that led me there.

I immediately looked up at the scoreboard. There was a number one next to my name.

I couldn't believe it.

I shattered the track record and won the gold medal by the largest margin in the history of the sport.

I had just become the World Champion.

I didn't win because the excuses disappeared. I won because I refused to let them decide my future.

THE STAIRS ARE ALWAYS WORKING

"Too often, we convince ourselves that massive success requires massive action."

James Clear said that. And he's right.

Your goals feel far away.
Unclear.
Overwhelming.

So, you wait.

You wait for the elevator to your goals.

You stand there. You stare at the numbers. You press the button over and over again. As if that might speed things up.

You glance at the stairs and consider them for about half a second. Then you remember what you want.

The big contract.
The instant weight loss.
The corner office.

And the stairs feel slow.

So, you turn back to the elevator. And you wait.

This is where we get it wrong. We assume change requires a big plan. A dramatic reset or a total life overhaul. But research shows the opposite.

Big overhauls usually fail. Not because people don't care. But because overwhelm shuts action down.

Meanwhile, 60 seconds pass. Then another. And another. Time keeps ticking whether you move forward or not.

The stairs were always working.

You're not stuck. You're just waiting for the wrong thing.

YOUR BRAIN NEEDS PROGRESS

Here's what most people miss.

The problem isn't the task, the goal, or the deadline. The problem is the moment you stop moving and start waiting.

Research from Harvard, led by Teresa Amabile and Steven Kramer, found something surprising. Motivation doesn't come from massive change, praise, bonuses, or even big wins.

It comes from progress.

Small, visible progress in meaningful work.

That's it.

When you move even a little, confidence rises and effort becomes easier to sustain. Not because life got easier, but because momentum showed up.

You think readiness comes first, but it doesn't. Action does.

Progress creates motivation. Which means the next 60 seconds matter more than the perfect plan. And if you're not convinced yet, listen to this.

WHY YAHOO MISSED THE MOMENT

At one point, Yahoo was one of the most powerful companies on the internet. Then leadership hesitated.

It lost its lead in search. Missed the rise of social media. Failed to capitalize on mobile.

In 2008, Yahoo turned down a $44.6 billion acquisition offer from Microsoft. They believed they were worth more, so leadership waited.

Eight years later, in 2016, Yahoo sold its core internet business to Verizon for $4.8 billion. That's nearly a 90 percent loss in value.

So, how does a company with that much talent and brand power fall so far behind?

The answer wasn't a lack of intelligence, or resources, or vision. It was much more tragic than that. They simply delayed decisions. Even Yahoo's CEO at the time, Marissa Mayer, pointed to hesitation.

Napoleon Hill said it plainly.

"The most dangerous enemy you will ever face is indecision."

Hesitation destroys companies. And lives. And dreams.

WHY ACTION WINS AT APPLE

While Yahoo was waiting for the elevator, Apple was taking the stairs. One step at a time.

Apple didn't become Apple because it planned longer. It became Apple because it decided faster.

Steve Jobs built a culture where the people closest to the work were expected to act. Not wait.

Decisions were made by experts. Not committees. And if something was off, it was addressed immediately. Not in the next quarter. Not after another round of meetings. Right then.

Tim Cook became CEO and continued that discipline.

Fewer projects. Clear priorities and fast decisions followed by immediate movement.

Because of that, Apple is now the most valuable company in the world, with a market value hovering around 3 trillion dollars.

And this is the part that most people miss.

Massive success doesn't come from massive plans. It comes from moments of execution, stacked back-to-back.

60 seconds of action beats 60 days of waiting. Every time.

YOUR MOVE

So, here's the real question.

What could change in your life if you stopped filling the next 60 seconds with excuses and started filling it with action?

You send the message, make the call, or take the step.

You ask the hard question or you start before you feel ready.

The only thing standing between excuses and execution is what you do next. Not someday. Not when you feel ready. But in the next 60 seconds.

The stairs are right there. They always were.

WHICH SIDE OF PROGRESS ARE YOU STANDING ON?

ADOBE VS CANVA

For years, if you were serious about design, you used Adobe. It was the gold standard. Power. Precision. Credibility. Entire industries depended on it and that kind of success teaches one lesson.

Protect what works.

So, Adobe did.

Then along came Melanie Perkins.

She was a student at the University of Western Australia, teaching basic design skills to other students. And she kept seeing the same thing happen.

Smart people. Capable people. Frozen at the first screen. Not because they lacked ideas, but because the tools felt overwhelming. The problem wasn't motivation. The problem was the complexity of it all.

So, Melanie and her then-boyfriend, now husband, Cliff Obrecht, built Canva.

Their goal was simple.

Shrink the first step. Fewer decisions. No learning curve before progress.

They pitched the idea again and again. And got rejected again and again. Walking away would have been reasonable but instead, they didn't give up.

Nearly 5 years after their first pitches, Canva launched. Today, it's one of the most widely used design platforms in the world. And I know exactly why, because I've lived it.

Years ago, I tried to design a birthday card for my daughter, Lacee, using Adobe. One hour later and 3 YouTube tutorials deep, I had created one balloon.

One.

Adobe is still world-class. It just wasn't built for beginners.

Now, my 10-year-old twins open Canva and build full scenes in seconds.

Balloons. Music. Elephants.

The works.

And here's the point.

When the first step feels simple, your brain doesn't freeze. It moves. And that matters more than we realize.

THE REAL JOB OF AN EXCUSE

Before we go any further, let's clear something up.

An excuse isn't a failure of character. It's just a defense mechanism.

Your brain is trying to protect you. Your identity. Your confidence.

Especially when action feels risky.

That's why excuses show up when something matters. And that's why they sound so reasonable.

I just need more time.
What if I mess up?
Someone else can do a better job than I can.

Each one lowers discomfort in the short term. And each one delays movement. On their own, they seem harmless. Responsible, even. But over time, those small justifications begin to slowly stack.

One reason. Then another. Then another. Until one day, you realize you are standing on the wrong side of your own progress.

YOU BUILD THE WALL ONE BRICK AT A TIME

Think of it this way.

The Great Wall of China wasn't built as one bold project.

It was built in fragments. Over centuries. By different dynasties responding to immediate threats.

Each section made sense at the time. Each addition felt protective.

But over time, the wall became a permanent barrier rather than a temporary defense.

That's how excuses work.

Each false story you tell yourself becomes a brick.

At first, that wall feels safe. It shields you from failure, judgment, and disappointment.

But "safety" slowly turns into "stuck."

You realize the wall isn't protecting you anymore. It's actually trapping you.

You wake up one day blocked from the life you want. You built a wall of excuses.

One accepted thought, and one brick at a time.

It wasn't my fault.
Not today.
When things calm down.

Historically, the Great Wall kept people out. Your personal wall keeps you in. And the irony is brutal.

What once felt like protection slowly becomes the thing that limits movement, growth, and freedom.

The only way over the excuses is by taking action. Immediate action. Within the first 60 seconds of the thought.

That's the ladder to the life you really want to live. That's how you climb up and over before hesitation has time to add another brick.

WHEN COURAGE MOVES FASTER THAN FEAR

60 SECONDS OF COURAGE

On January 15, 2009, U.S. Airways Flight 1549 lifted off from LaGuardia Airport in New York City. Captain Chesley "Sully" Sullenberger and First Officer Jeff Skiles were in the cockpit.

Within minutes, a flock of geese struck both engines and the plane lost all power at 2,800 feet.

They had no thrust. No altitude. No time.

Investigators later determined that Sully had less than 60 seconds to decide the fate of everyone on board.

He could risk turning back toward LaGuardia or attempt to land in New Jersey. Air traffic control urged him to return but the data said he wouldn't make it.

His instruments screamed warnings. But Sully didn't have the luxury of time or analysis.

He had to act.

With years of experience and instinct sharpened by repetition, Sully made a decision that defied protocol and saved 155 lives.

He leveled the plane. Calculated his glide and chose a third option.

The Hudson River.

In interviews afterward, Sully said,

"I don't remember hearing the birds. I remember the silence after impact."

That silence came in the seconds immediately following the bird strike, when both engines went quiet and he realized the gravity of what had happened.

It was in that silence that courage took over.

Less than 4 minutes after engine failure, Flight 1549 rested safely on the water.

It became one of the most remarkable emergency landings in aviation history.

WHAT HAPPENS WHEN YOU HESITATE

Now ask yourself this.

What if Sully had waited to make a decision?

What if he had let fear whisper, *"You've never done this before. You can't do this."*

In those few seconds, hesitation could have changed everything.

Fear crashes far more than airplanes.

It quietly derails potential.
Relationships.
Dreams.

So let me ask you.

Where are your engines stalling right now?
What risks are you avoiding?
If you keep hesitating, where does that land you?

Because the most dangerous moment isn't when everything goes wrong.
It's when waiting would make perfect sense.

MINUTE TO WIN-IT

At family parties, we sometimes play Minute to Win It games and it's amazing how fast the energy in the room changes when that timer starts.

You've experienced this.

One minute you're sitting there, comfortable, watching everyone else in a room.

The next minute, your name is called and you're jumping around trying to shake ping pong balls out of a tissue box strapped to your backside like your life depends on it.

Dignity gone. Focus locked in.

In that 60-second window, energy spikes and everything narrows.

Life works the same way.

One minute can completely change your energy. One minute can win your day.

THE THING YOU HAVEN'T DONE YET

So let me ask you something. What excuse are you making today?

Just pick one.

This week, I had 17 texts come in at once. But I told myself I'd reply later. That felt reasonable.

Well, it's been 3 days. Now those 17 messages have become a full-on situation. What started as a small delay has officially become an excuse.

We all have something like this.

A task that isn't big but somehow gets heavier the longer you wait. The cold leads you haven't touched. The apology you owe. The bedtime you keep delaying.

Every minute you postpone, the brick wall gets taller.

Catch yourself right there. That's your moment to move.

THE 60 SECONDS CHALLENGE

Do this with me.

Set a timer for 60 seconds and do "the thing." Or at least start.

Obviously, one minute won't allow me to respond to 17 texts. But I can answer 2. And that's enough to break the barrier.

The goal isn't to finish everything. The goal is to prove to your brain that action is safe.

You've got one minute.

Send one text. Take one step. Put away one thing.

Pause the reading here.

Go.

...

...

The second you start moving, your brain switches from "protect" to progress. And courage always follows motion.

If you did this, you felt it.

The task feels smaller.
Your energy is higher.

Remember that feeling because that's evidence that you can trust yourself to follow through.

One minute to move. One minute to act.

If someone comes to mind, text them. If an idea sparks, write it down. If you see a need, take one small step toward it.

Do this every day and you start becoming the person you say you want to be.

The 60 Seconds Challenge isn't about doing more. It's about doing it sooner.

MOVE AWAY FROM BEING STUCK

When COVID hit in 2020, my husband Janson and I found ourselves waiting.

Waiting for work. Waiting for phone calls. Waiting for something. Anything. To get better.

Our business relies on keynote speaking and corporate training. And both disappeared overnight.

We told ourselves what people always tell themselves in moments like that.

"This is just how it is."
"There's nothing we can do."
"Maybe we should give up on this plan."

Every excuse sounded logical. They almost always do.

Then I came across a quote from General George S. Patton:

"A good plan, violently executed now, is better than a perfect plan executed next week."

I printed it and taped it to our office wall.

That was the moment we stopped waiting and started creating.

Janson and I tore apart a bedroom in our basement and turned it into a makeshift virtual studio.

It wasn't perfect, but it moved us away from being stuck.

That single decision led to new clients, events, and financial stability.

That's how fast change can happen. It's usually one decision away. Not when everything's ready. But when you are.

DIFFERENT STORIES. SAME RULE.

Across every successful story, the pattern is the same.

Action wins.

Apple didn't wait for perfect information. It decided quickly and trusted momentum to teach what planning couldn't.

Canva didn't wait for permission. It simplified and stepped up.

Sully didn't wait for certainty. He acted in seconds and saved lives.

And when COVID shut everything down, waiting would have felt reasonable, but movement opened doors.

In each of these cases, progress didn't come from bigger plans. It came from immediate decisions. From using the next 60 seconds to move instead of explain.

What you do in the next minute shapes your life. Your leadership. And your results.

START, THEN ADJUST

Zig Ziglar said it best.

"You don't have to be great to start, but you have to start to be great."

And yet, this is exactly where most people stall.

They wait to begin their life.
They wait to lead.
They wait for things to feel perfect.

But success doesn't come from waiting. It comes from action.

From starting.
From taking risks.
From adjusting throughout minutes of your day.

It's about choosing to learn as you go.

And that's exactly how you race in skeleton.

You start.
Then you adjust in real time.

One choice here.
One correction there.

That race in St. Moritz looked like it was decided in one minute on the ice. But it wasn't.

It was decided in the unseen moments before. The moments when my mind tried to slow me down. And I chose to go anyway.

I didn't wait for the elevator on the path to becoming a World Champion. I took the stairs.

One small step.
Then another.
Then another.

THE NEXT MINUTE IS YOURS

Living with **"NO EXCUSES"** doesn't mean living a perfect life.

It means being willing to try. And being willing to improve.

That's it.

NO EXCUSES.

Take ownership of your life. Your thoughts. Your effort.

Own it.

Do what you say you'll do. Be who you say you want to be. One minute is long enough to change your direction.

Stop waiting for the elevator. Take the stairs.

Text back. Clean the counter. Apologize. Pray. Do one thing. Just move.

The life you want doesn't start someday. It starts in the next 60 seconds.

CHAPTER 6

If Nothing Changes...

"If you keep doing what you're doing,
you'll keep getting what you're getting."
—*Tim Ferriss*

STOP BLAMING THE TRACK

ALTENBERG, GERMANY.

Just saying the name made veterans flinch.

There are two major lessons that I learned on this track.

The first lesson came in my first season on the World Cup team. And the second lesson came in my final season.

Remember, this track is known as the most dangerous track in the world.

I heard the horror stories and warnings about this place the first day I began sliding. A twisting descent carved through unforgiving walls of concrete and ice.

"It's a beast."
"Altenberg will chew you up."
"Dude. You're gonna eat it when you go there."

I'll never forget my first race there. Our team showed up to the Eastern German track, anxious and full of fear. Turns out, we had every reason to feel that way. 6 athletes ended up in the hospital that first day of training. And I hit the roof hard. But I managed to avoid getting in the ambulance to the vet hospital.

Then race day came 3 days later.

The green light flashed for my World Cup debut.

I sprinted, dove headfirst onto my sled, and felt the ice scrape beneath me. Every corner demanded precision. Movements from my shoulders and pressure through my knees steered my course.

When I crossed the finish line, I looked up and was stoked to see a ninth-place finish beside my name.

But before I could celebrate, everyone was already blaming the track. Corners 4, 9, 10, and 12 apparently ruined everyone's run. I didn't want to be left out and I sure didn't want to think that my great finish was only because theirs were so terrible.

So, I joined in.

"Yeah, corner 10 wrecked me and I slammed out of corner 12. I could've done better, but the track wouldn't let me."

I exaggerated the heck out of it.

You've done this too.

Maybe not on an ice track, but somewhere in your life.

You've blamed the bad Wi-Fi, the broken printer, or the noise in the office that's keeping you from doing your job. Because most of the time, it feels better to point at something else than to own the outcome.

That day, I learned something about excuses.

They feel good. Really good.

Each one was like a sigh of relief, a way to release the pressure and feel safe again.

I made the top ten in my World Cup debut. The best result of my rookie season. But obviously, it was the track that didn't let me do better.

I REALLY HATE THIS PLACE

Altenberg was on the schedule again the following year.

I couldn't escape the feeling of panic in my chest.

The plane landed. We drove up the mountain. And the team's dread sank into my mind like a rock in a pond.

Doubts. Frustration. Chatter.

"I really hate this place."
"Hope I survive."
"This track is so dangerous."

Even though I had my best finish here the previous season, the negative energy around me was contagious.

By the time I unpacked my sled, I was repeating their words out loud. So, when it was my turn to go, I raced with one soundtrack looping in my head.

I hate this track.
I hate this track.

19 corners. One mile of ice.

I crossed the finish line in 1:02.91 and looked up at the scoreboard.

Ninth place. Again.

I blamed the ice. The track. The weather. The equipment.

Anything but me.

This time, I even blamed the doughnut stand outside of corner 9. True story. The smell was so sweet I told my coach it threw me off. Our team was sure the Germans placed it there on purpose.

It sure made me feel better to know that my result wasn't my fault.

EXPECTING DIFFERENT RESULTS

A couple of years passed, and I returned to Altenberg once again. This time, as the World Champion.

Older. Wiser. Tougher.

I worked harder than before. I studied the track endlessly. I watched how the Germans moved. Every micro-shift of a shoulder, every ounce of pressure through a knee.

I was ready to stare down the beast that had beaten me before. I still hated the track. But this time I was coming for it.

My goal was simple.

Stand on the podium in Altenberg.

Race day came and my name echoed through the speakers. At the start line, I tightened my gloves, strapped my helmet, and focused on the goal in front of me.

This was it. This was the day everything would change.

I took a deep breath and exhaled just before pushing off.

Poof.

In that single breath, my visor fogged. Completely.

Within seconds, the moisture froze into a spiderweb of ice crystals. I could literally see the ice spreading across my visor until everything blurred.

Each second, I waited, my vision shrank smaller and smaller.

5 seconds to start. No time to think.

I couldn't see but thought,

"It is what it is. Just go."

So, I went.

It's like turning off your GPS halfway through downtown Boston and thinking, *'Yeah, i'll just wing it.'*

...But slightly worse.

Headfirst. 80 miles an hour. Blind.

Every instinct in me said, *"Get off the sled."*

I felt the fear, and I mean I felt it.

It wasn't just a flicker of doubt. The fear went straight to my chest like icy water dumped straight into my lungs

The ice crystals kept spreading. I gripped the handles so tight my knuckles ached. I slammed the walls in 4, 9, and 10, just like always.

When I crossed the finish line, out of breath and amazed that I made it down alive, I ripped off my helmet and saw it.

Ninth place. Again.

I couldn't believe it. The result would never change.

Same track.
Same fear.
Same outcome.

And once again, I blamed the track.

You blame your "tracks," too.

The lost sale.
The never changing day.
The same argument on repeat.

But the only thing you can really control is how you handle the ride and what you carry with you along the way.

My real problem wasn't the ice on my visor. It was the mental fog I'd let settle in.

Excuses had been clouding my vision one thin layer at a time. The fear. The negative self-talk. The mind games.

Every time I blamed someone or something, I lost sight of who I wanted to be.

THE EXCUSES STOP HERE

Fast forward to the end of my career. I was one season away from retirement.

The summer before the sliding season began, the itinerary was posted. I looked at the World Cup schedule and my heart sank.

Altenberg.

Again.

"Seriously? Any track but Altenberg."

Einstein once said insanity is doing the same thing over and over and expecting a different result. I definitely expected different results, but I was trapped in my own thinking.

The track.
The corners.

Nothing would change.

I thought back to that day when my visor fogged. My vision was gone. And I still blamed the track.

The irony?

I couldn't see the ice. And I couldn't see the truth either.

And then it hit me. Hard.

You can't fix a problem that you refuse to see. And I'd refused to see the real one.

It wasn't the track.
It was me.
Nothing changed because I hadn't.

So, I asked myself a different question.

If the track won't change, what do I need to do differently?

The answer was uncomfortable. And obvious.

Stop blaming the track. Just change the way you see it.

That was my turning point. I would choose to see it differently.

I decided Altenberg would become my favorite track in the world. Even if I had to trick my brain into believing it.

It wouldn't be easy. It wouldn't be comfortable. But I was tired of being stuck. Discomfort had to be better than defeat.

So, I studied. I analyzed. I learned.

I watched the film at 5000 frames per second. Hours of it. Every curve. Every line. Every movement. And I stopped seeing Corner 10 as a deathtrap and started seeing it as a teacher.

I gamified the fear.

When the butterflies hit, I told myself, *"That's not anxiety. That's just excitement. You don't HAVE to do this. You GET to."*

The track stopped being my enemy. It became my training partner. The more I respected it, the less power it had over me.

And then something unexpected happened.

I started looking forward to competing in Altenberg. And when I changed how I saw the track, I started seeing everything in my life differently.

I learned that vision isn't just about seeing where you're going. It's about knowing who you are.

So, I surrounded myself with influences that reflected who I wanted to become.

Music that lifted me.
Books that stretched me.

When negative conversations showed up, I redirected them. And if that didn't work, I put on my headphones and turned on Enya. Or I simply stepped away.

I stopped relying on willpower and I built my world to make success inevitable.

You can't always control the noise around you, but you *can choose* whether you stay in it.

Maybe for you it isn't a sled track.

Maybe it's endless scrolling that convinces you everyone else is winning.
The influences you haven't questioned yet.
A podcast that leaves you anxious instead of inspired.

The moment you notice what lifts you up and what drags you down is the moment you get to choose what happens next.

CHANGE THE WAY YOU SEE IT

When I arrived in Altenberg for the last time, I was ready.

I could finally *see* where I wanted to go.

Nothing about Altenberg had changed. But everything within me had.

For the first time, I had a clear vision. Not just of where I was going, but of *who I was becoming.*

I no longer fought the track. I worked with it. I maneuvered through each corner with a calm awareness like a chess player who finally understands the board.

The smell of doughnuts out of corner 9 didn't faze me. I even grabbed a plate after the race.

Corner 10 finally made sense. And 12 was smooth as butter.

When I crossed the finish line and looked up, the number beside my name wasn't 9.

It was 3.
Third place.
A podium finish on the track that once confined me.

I lifted my head, tears blurring my eyes, and thought,

It worked!

That bronze medal meant more than all the gold ones that season. Because it wasn't just a race result that changed.

It was *me.*

NOTHING CHANGES UNLESS YOU DO

If stepping outside your comfort zone feels so good after you do it, why don't you do it more often?

Just like I was blindly sliding down the Altenberg track, we're often blind to the small things keeping us stuck.

The messes that slowly pile up.
The habits that lead us away from good things.
The excuses that whisper, "It's fine. I'm fine."

You've been here.

When you think, "I'll just scroll for a minute," and suddenly you know the life story of a stranger's dog.

There's actually a name for this.

It's called **Change Blindness**.

Your brain is wired to ignore gradual decline. So, it adapts slowly to a slightly worse job, a declining relationship, or a poor health habit.

You don't even notice it's happening. You think you'll recognize when things get bad enough to change. But guess what? You won't.

By the time you feel it, you're already deep in the boiling pot.

THE BOILING FROG WAKE-UP CALL

You know the story.

Drop a frog in cool water, turn up the heat slowly, and it never jumps out.

That poor frog doesn't jump because the temperature rises just one degree at a time.

That's you.
That's me.
That's anyone tolerating a one-degree increase of unhappiness each day.

You adapt to the endless projects that you start but never finish. You adapt to the relationship that steals your joy. You adapt to one degree of stress, pain, or toxicity every single day until you are cooked at 212 degrees Fahrenheit.

Then you wonder, *how did I get here?*

So, ask yourself this.

Are you living your dream life, or are you sitting in that pot?

THE FROZEN YEAR

I want you to imagine something for a minute.

What if you had to live today on repeat for the rest of your life?

You wake up tomorrow, and it's the same morning as today. Just like the classic movie *Groundhog Day*. But make it your actual Tuesday.

Same morning routine.
Same job.
Same habits.

The tone you used with your kids, your coworker, or the person who cut you off on the freeway.

That's who you'll continue to be.

No growth.
No progress.
No change.

Just this day.
On repeat.

Would you be okay with this? Really think about it.

Because if you don't change what you're doing today, this is exactly what your future will look like.

One year from now, if nothing changes, you'll have the same arguments, the same habits, the same worries, and the same excuses.

Pain isn't the enemy. Staying the same is.

IF YOU DON'T CHANGE, NOTHING WILL

I heard a quote once that stuck with me.

"Growth is painful. Change is painful. But nothing is as painful as staying stuck somewhere you don't belong."

That's the truth you've been avoiding.

You're not waiting for the right time. You're waiting for clarity. And until then, your comfort is keeping you frozen.

Even the greats get blindsided by this. Take tennis star Andre Agassi, for example. Although he had won 3 Grand Slam titles and earned millions by 24, he was miserable.

"I hate tennis," he admitted.

He wasn't lazy or broken. He'd simply lost sight of what mattered. But when he tied his career to helping kids through his foundation, everything shifted. And his passion returned.

It wasn't the game that changed. It was him.

Here's the hard truth.

Your situation won't change until you do. And every change starts with one choice. The choice to stop making excuses.

So, what would your life look like if you didn't make excuses?

That's where we're going next.

The life you want is waiting for you to know exactly what you want. And then choose it.

LIFE WITHOUT EXCUSES

I want you to imagine living one full day with zero excuses.

Picture being the **absolute best** version of yourself.

What would this day look like?

Let's start the day now.

The alarm goes off.
Light filters in.
You stretch before your feet hit the floor.
You feel it.
There's purpose in your life.

Now see yourself at work, at home, or wherever you spend your day.

This is the day you finally throw the fishing line in the river.
You ask for that raise.
Go for a run.
Host that neighborhood dinner you've been talking about for years.
Or maybe you finally let yourself do nothing. And actually, enjoy it.

What does it look like when you stop overthinking and just take the first step you've been avoiding?

Picture the moments that test you.
A coworker frustrates you.
Plans fall apart.

How does the **NO EXCUSES** version of you respond?

Visualize yourself pausing, breathing, and choosing peace.

Now look around your life.

Your family.
Your friends.
The people you pass each day.

You stop comparing.
Stop judging.
Stop trying to keep score.

You begin serving others and start showing gratitude.

Take a breath.
Picture it.

Do you feel that shift?

Today is the day you really listen when your kid talks to you. You go on that hike, finish that project, or shut off your phone and be fully present.

At the end of the day, do you decide you want to wake up earlier tomorrow?

Or perhaps your body and mind need some deserved rest.

You ask yourself, *"How do I really want to use my time? Who do I truly want to be?"*

When you live without excuses, your relationships start to reflect it.

The energy changes.
The conversations change.

You change.

Take a second and let this version of you sink in.

PUT IT ON PAPER

Now grab something to write on.

I like to use butcher paper and colorful markers from my kids' art supplies, but anything will work.

At the top, in big, bold letters, write:

LIFE WITHOUT EXCUSES

Then ask yourself, *"What would it look like to live my life without excuses?"*

Don't overthink it.
Just start.

Picture your day again, hour by hour.

What does *that* version of you do differently?

Maybe living with **NO EXCUSES** means choosing yogurt over a donut.

Maybe it means saying yes to that 9 p.m. date with your spouse, even if you love being in pajamas by 7 P.M. (I do too.)

Maybe it's hitting your quota, forgiving the coworker who made you look bad, or setting aside time each week to play pickleball with friends.

Whatever it looks like, write it down. Make it true to you.

Let it be messy.
Doodle.
Scribble.

Take as much time as you need to do this.

Once you're finished, look at it.

When you see your life written out in front of you, without the weight of excuses, something inside you shifts.

You start to want that life.
You start to believe you can have it.
And the best part?

You can.

That's what Altenberg did for me.

It allowed me to see the life I wanted instead of staying trapped in the one I was living.

You don't need a perfect plan. You just need the willingness to try.

This is what it looks like to live with **NO EXCUSES**.

And once you see what you want, I mean really see it with vulnerable and honest eyes, you'll never want to live any other way.

THE POWER OF ONE THING

Here's a secret that all the greats understand.

Keep it simple.

David Brailsford. Kobe Bryant. Warren Buffett.

They didn't chase greatness. They broke it down.
Small steps. Clear focus. Relentless repetition.

And Mozart understood this too.

Yes, he was a genius. But he also worked like one. He once said, *"The shortest way to do many things is to do only one thing at a time."*

Which, let's be honest, isn't how most of us operate. We're out here juggling 20 tabs, 6 goals, and a load of laundry, wondering why we're exhausted.

But there's truth here.

He didn't write an entire symphony overnight. He focused on one measure. One line. One tiny part.

Again.
And again.
Until it became automatic.

YOUR PAPER, YOUR LIFE

You just made a blueprint of a "Life Without Excuses." It's *your* blueprint. It doesn't look like anyone else's because it's not supposed to.

This is your life. Your vision. Your symphony.

Now it's time to bring it to reality.

Take a look at your paper. All those ideas, dreams, habits, and shifts waiting to happen.

Now circle one thing.

Not 10. Not 5. Just one. The one that matters most right now.

Circle it big. Make it bold.

This is your non-negotiable.

Hang the paper where you'll see it every day. This isn't a decoration. It's a decision. A daily reminder of who you're becoming and what you're done excusing.

THE 60-SECOND WINDOW

Researchers say up to 95 percent of what you do every day is automatic.

Think about that. 95 percent of your thoughts, habits, and reactions happen on autopilot. So, if every day feels the same, it's because it is.

But when you change one thing, that percentage drops. You start living more intentionally.

When you feel that tug to act, to put the mulch down, to call your mom, or to finally schedule that overdue appointment, you have less than 60 seconds before your brain talks you out of it.

That's your window. The space between wanting to change and actually doing something about it.

If you move inside that window, you win. If you wait, the excuse wins.

Every single time.

PROVE IT TO YOURSELF

Now prove it.

If you can do your "one thing" right now, do it.

Make the phone call.
Send the email.
Schedule the appointment.

If you can't do it now, set an alarm for later today. Not next week. Not when things slow down.

When the alarm goes off, act.

NO EXCUSES.

Because the moment you move, even once, your life starts to change and excuses fade away.

Each 60-second decision you make is a vote for your future self, the one who doesn't wait, doesn't justify, and doesn't make excuses.

Don't wait any longer to start living your life. Don't wait for tomorrow. Or Monday. Just start now.

BE THE PERSON WHO DOES THE WORK

Every action you take or don't take is shaping who you are.

The goal is to change.
To become better.
To constantly improve.

Make today the day you take control of your life and become the kind of person who doesn't make excuses.

Before this book was even a thought, I asked myself, *"Who do I want to be?"*

3 answers came to mind.

I want to be someone who writes, someone who mountain bikes and someone who lives without excuses.

These identities will shift over time but that moment helped shape my blueprint.

"I'M A WRITER"

For years, I said, *"I want to write a book."* But "wanting" is the language of excuses.

I told myself I didn't have enough time, energy, or experience.

The truth was, I didn't believe I was a writer. Writers were people with literature degrees. Perfect grammar. Fancy words.

Then I remembered something James Clear wrote in *Atomic Habits*: *"Every action is a vote for the type of person you want to become."*

So, I started voting.

I decided to write a news article every week, no matter what. Some weeks the words came easily. Other weeks, they fought me every sentence.

But I kept writing.

Eventually, something shifted.

I stopped saying, *"I want to be a writer,"* and started saying, *"I'm a writer."*

That was it. That was the moment I really became one.

"I'M A MOUNTAIN BIKER."

Same script. New setting.

My kids joined the high school mountain biking team, and of course, I was all in. When they dive into something, I can't help but follow.

Only problem?

I'd never been on a mountain bike before. Not once. I had no idea what I was doing. And every excuse came rushing in.

I told myself I didn't belong on the trails. I thought, *"I'll look ridiculous. I don't even know how to ride on dirt. I'll go next time."*

Then one evening, I caught myself mid-excuse. And that pause mattered. Because I realized something simple and uncomfortable.

If I didn't interrupt the thought, I'd live inside it.

So, I did the only thing that would force action. I got my bike and gear ready for a morning ride. No debate. No escape hatch.

I said, *"I'm a mountain biker."*

Did I suddenly have confidence? Nope. But that sentence got me out the door.

I didn't have to be good. I just had to start pedaling.

"I DON'T MAKE EXCUSES."

Yesterday reminded me of this again.

I walked up my parents' path to work on this book. Our motorhome is parked beside their house so that I can write without constant interruptions from my 4 amazing kiddos.

I was juggling a box, my water flask, and my laptop. The branches from an old tree had been blocking the walkway for months.

Dad pushed them aside to pass. Too feeble to fix the problem himself. Mom took the long way around the house to avoid it.

I sighed. *"I don't have time for this."*

And then I stopped. Because I remembered who I decided to be.

"NO EXCUSES, Noelle. Just get it done."

I set everything down. Walked to the shed. Grabbed Dad's handheld chainsaw.

Ten minutes later, the path was clear.

Dad's hug said everything.

Nothing changes if nothing changes. Obstacles don't move themselves.

Sometimes clearing your own path means setting down all the things you're holding onto and deciding you won't walk around the problem anymore.

That's what living with **NO EXCUSES** actually looks like.

You start seeing obstacles differently. They stop being reasons to hold back and start becoming proof that you're capable of more.

SEE IT. OWN IT. DO IT.

If your days feel the same, and your months blur together, remember Altenberg.

The track didn't change.

I did.

Stop blaming the track. And change the way you see the problems around you.

Each time you say you want to live without excuses, you'll start making better decisions in your life. Your teams will rise to the standard. And your results will show.

And yes, it'll get hard.

Motivation will fade. That's normal. But your purpose will steady you. Purpose is what pulls you forward when motivation taps out.

When your why is strong enough, the how will always find a way.

So, the next time you hear that whisper,

I'll do it later...

Catch it.
Smile.
And say, "No. I don't make excuses."

Then move.

CHAPTER 7

Purpose in Real Time

"People lose their way when they lose their why."
—*Simon Sinek*

THE STREET WHERE MY OLYMPIC DREAM BEGAN

Everyone has a place where a dream began.

Maybe it was the hallway in your childhood home where posters covered the walls. Or the cubicle where you realized, *"I can't spend the rest of my life doing this."* Maybe it was your kitchen table at 2 a.m., sitting with a notebook and a whole lot of hope.

For me, it happened on a street that ran straight through Pocatello, Idaho.

I was a freshman competing in track and field for the University of Utah. It was February 2002, and we had just finished a competition inside Idaho State University's dome.

Back home, our campus had been turned into the Olympic Village for the Salt Lake City Games, so our team had been temporarily relocated to Idaho.

I competed well that day.
Strong jumps. Solid throws. A good race.

More importantly, I felt it. I felt myself becoming the athlete I wanted to be.

When we got back to the hotel, I ran straight to the TV.

I dropped to my knees on the carpet. Flipping through channels like a kid hoping to watch cartoons on Saturday morning. My face just inches from the screen.

The Olympic Games were on, and I didn't want to miss a second. This was the day that skeleton returned to the Olympic Games after 54 years.

I turned the volume up just in time to see it.

Lea Ann Parsley won silver.
And Tristan Gale won gold.

I knew both of them.

Pride rushed through me for our country. Awe hit me as I watched women I had trained beside live their dream. But more than anything, I felt a certainty settle deep within me.

"That's gonna be me. In 4 years, I'm gonna be an Olympian."

The day before I would have said my goal was to have fun. But that day, everything changed.

I didn't want to just compete.
I wanted to be the best in the world.

As my eyes closed that night in the Best Western at 1415 Bench Road in Pocatello, Idaho, my purpose for doing skeleton became crystal clear.

"I'm going to stand on that podium."

TORINO 2006 - WHEN PURPOSE BREAKS

4 years later, I wasn't the girl glued to the TV anymore.

I was ranked number one in the world in skeleton.

I didn't hope I could win. I knew I could. But purpose can be fragile when life hits you sideways.

During our Olympic Trials, a 4-man bobsled flew out of the track and slammed into me.

I never saw it coming.

It shattered my leg. And it shattered my Olympic dream. And my purpose vanished in an instant.

We all know that hit. The one that knocks the breath out of you. The one that forces you to rebuild whether you want to or not.

This is the part we rarely talk about.

Sometimes your purpose doesn't change because you get distracted or unfocused. Sometimes it changes because life blindsides you and forces you into a reality you never asked for.

I wanted to compete so badly. But instead, I was back in front of a television screen. It was a different street. But I knew I was back in the same place my Olympic dream had begun 4 years earlier.

I watched Switzerland, Great Britain, and Canada stand on the Olympic podium. And I felt the ache of knowing I was supposed to be there.

VANCOUVER 2010 - I DIDN'T JUST LOSE. I WAS LOST.

The following year, I came back with a fire I'd never felt before and won the World Championships. It looked like the perfect comeback on paper.

But inside, I was exhausted and empty.

The mental and emotional strain of returning after the bobsled accident took everything out of me.

So, I stepped away.

I needed distance from the sport that had become a battlefield.

I took a year off.
We had our baby girl.
And I loved being home.

I still planned to return for the 2010 Olympics. But beneath that plan was a quieter truth.

I didn't know if I could do it anymore.
And I didn't know if I *wanted* to.

Trauma rewires you. It changes how you show up to the things you once loved. If you've ever stood in a familiar place and felt like a stranger, then you know exactly what I mean.

When I returned to skeleton for the Vancouver Games, I wasn't racing toward a dream.

I was surviving.

Every airport was another goodbye to my daughter. Every training day came with guilt.

My purpose wasn't strong enough to carry me through and I was miserable. And without a solid purpose, even the Olympics feels heavy.

I crossed the finish line in the absolute worst position an athlete can land.

Fourth place.
One-tenth of a second from the podium.
And in the interviews immediately following the race, I laughed.

Not from joy. But from relief.
It was over.
I could finally go home.

SOCHI 2014 - "MOMENT OF THE GAMES"

After Vancouver, I retired and felt nothing but relief. For the first time in years, my life finally slowed down.

I was home.
I made strawberry jam.
I sewed the T-shirt quilt I had been saving for "someday."

We welcomed our son, Traycen, in 2011, and skeleton racing faded so far into the background that it didn't even cross my mind. I thought that chapter of my life had closed forever.

And then the unthinkable happened.

In April of 2012, at 18 weeks pregnant, our baby girl's heart stopped beating.

I was rushed to the emergency room and I miscarried. The doctors tried to save her, but in the end, they were fighting to save me.

When I got home from the hospital, the grief swallowed me whole.

Sadness.
Confusion.
Despair.

It pressed in from every direction and followed me everywhere.

My husband saw it. He saw the light fading. He knew I needed something to hope for again. Something that could lift me out of the darkness.

One afternoon, 2 months later, he walked into our bedroom. He sat down beside me, and said,

"Noelle, this has been really hard on both of us. I've been thinking about how to move forward. What if you went back?"

My head was shaking before he finished the sentence.
He saw my walls go up instantly. So, he leaned forward and said,

"But this time, what if we did it together as a family?"

Time stood still for a moment.

You've been here too.

The moment when staying the same feels safe, but choosing the unknown could change your entire life. You don't know where the choice leads. You just know it could open a future you never imagined you were allowed to have.

He knew I hadn't retired because I couldn't compete. I retired because I couldn't keep leaving my family.

Something inside me shifted.
A new purpose sparked to life.
I thought about what that would really mean.

"What if this time, we could chase the dream together?"

I felt hope rise in a way I hadn't felt in years.
Excitement. Wonder. Direction.

But mostly, I finally had a purpose to get out of bed and move forward.

That conversation and decision changed our future.

I immediately created a plan. I was going to get stronger. Faster. Better. Because now my purpose wasn't about me anymore.

It was about us.

For the next 2 years, my husband, 2 children, and I traveled the world together.

One country.
One hotel room.
One race at a time.

I came back sprinting faster than I had as a Division I athlete.

My mind was strong. My body was ready. And in those 2 seasons, I won more individual gold medals than any country's athletes combined.

I crossed the finish line at the Olympic Games in second place. A silver medal.

To some, that may have been a disappointing finish. But fortunately for me, I didn't allow anyone else's definition of success to define my own.

I knew why I was there.

I jumped into the stands, wrapped my arms around my husband and children, and shouted,

"We did it! We did it! "

Because that medal wasn't mine.

It was ours.

That moment, filled with intention, alignment, and purpose, was later named the *Moment of the 2014 Winter Olympic Games* by the United States Olympic and Paralympic Committee.

Pure joy came from that race. And that joy came from following my purpose.

That moment was so much more than I could have imagined or hoped for.

DIFFERENT DAY, DIFFERENT PURPOSE

My purpose didn't stay the same over the years.

It sharpened.
It broke.
It was rebuilt.

The clearer it was, the more committed I became.

But here's the point.

Purpose has layers.

The deep, lifelong purpose usually stays steady. But the day-to-day and season-to-season purpose shifts as your life shifts.

Purpose is allowed to evolve because you are allowed to evolve. But when purpose disappears, like it did for me in 2010, excuses start running your life for you.

NO PURPOSE, NO PROGRESS

AARON BURR

In the musical *Hamilton*, Aaron Burr is the man who spends his entire life waiting for the perfect moment.

He's brilliant, connected, and capable of greatness, but he never chooses a direction.

He keeps his head down, smiles politely, and watches everyone else take risks while he waits for certainty that never comes.

He wants influence but refuses to take a stand.
He wants opportunity but runs from commitment.
He wants purpose but avoids choosing one.

Throughout the musical, he repeats,

"I'm willing to wait for it. Wait for it. Wait for it."

These aren't virtues. They're excuses.

His "waiting" becomes procrastination.
His "smiling" becomes a mask.
His "patience" becomes paralysis.

Burr falls into every Excuser type you and I have ever faced.

He avoids decisions.
He blames circumstances.
He justifies every delay.
He doubts his readiness.
He tries to please everyone but himself.

He spent so much time saying yes to the safe things that he never said yes to the decisions that would have given his life meaning.

He chased the good and missed the best. And it cost him everything.

When you don't stand for something, you don't move toward anything.

Burr's excuses didn't just slow him down. They destroyed the very future he claimed he wanted.

IF IT'S EVERYTHING, IT'S NOTHING

If everything feels important, nothing feels clear.

You feel pulled in a hundred directions. Every request sounds reasonable. Every opportunity feels like it matters. And slowly, without realizing it, your purpose gets diluted.

One of our family's favorite movies is Disney's *The Incredibles*. There's a line from the villain, Syndrome, that always makes me laugh because it's painfully true.

"And when everyone's super... no one will be."

That line nails it. If everything is important, nothing is.

This is exactly what Greg McKeown teaches in his work on leadership and decision-making. Purpose is built on trade-offs.

You can't pursue everything and expect clarity. You can't say yes to every request and still live with direction.

Purpose demands elimination. It asks you to choose the vital few and release the trivial many.

MAKE SPACE FOR YOU

Think of your life like that overstuffed closet you keep calling "organized," even though it's one bad hinge away from taking you out.

It's packed with jeans from 2003, mismatched socks, and "someday" hobbies.

And because it's crammed with old identity clutter, you can't see what fits you now.

So, pull it all out.

Unload the commitments you said yes to just to avoid an awkward moment.
Eliminate the goals you've dragged behind for years. Remove the expectations you inherited but never chose.

Look at your calendar, your schedule, and your to-do lists.

Hold each one up and ask, "Does this fit who I am today?"

If it doesn't, it's gone.

It's time for a fresh start.

You can't grow into the person you want to become if your closet is still hoarding your past.

REGRET HITS HARDER

Your life shrinks or expands based on the decisions you're willing to make. Put them off long enough, and regret becomes the one calling the shots.

And here's the simple truth.

Discipline is hard.
But regret is harder.

No one proves this better than Aaron Burr.

He waited.
He hesitated.
He filled his life with the clutter of safe choices until regret was the only thing left.

Purpose demands discipline. It asks you to stand for something.

The work is uncomfortable.

But so is living someone else's life.

WHEN YESTERDAY'S PURPOSE ISN'T THE SAME AS TODAY'S

By the early 2000s, LEGO was collapsing under its own confusion. They were everywhere except where they were strongest.

Theme parks. Clothing lines. Video games. And over $800 million in debt. The brand was drowning in distractions.

Then Jørgen Vig Knudstorp stepped in as CEO and made one bold decision.

"We go back to what we do best, and we choose to be the best at building bricks."

Period.

He cut the clutter. He killed the noise. He brought the company back to its core.

'Inspiring creativity through building.'

And everything shifted.

The culture realigned.
The products were refined.
And the identity snapped back into place.

The moment they reclaimed what mattered, momentum returned. And within a decade, LEGO became one of the most powerful brands on earth.

60-SECOND CHALLENGE - CHECK IN WITH YOURSELF

Just like LEGO had to redefine what mattered most, you have to do the same.

Purpose only works when it matches the season, you're in right now. And let's be honest. Most of us never stop long enough to ask what we're actually doing with our lives.

We wake up, check our phones, race through mornings we barely remember, sit in countless meetings, and wonder why we feel stuck.

So let me ask you directly.

What's your purpose?
Why are you showing up the way you do every day?

And don't give me yesterday's answer.

Yesterday's purpose might not fit today's life.

Maybe today's purpose is rebuilding your confidence.
Maybe it's being more present with your family.
Or protecting your health because stress is starting to show up in ways you can't ignore.

Here's your 60-second challenge. Take one minute and answer this.

What matters right now?

Name it.

Write it down.

Let it shape your decisions today.

SHACKLETON AND THE *ENDURANCE*

One of the books I tell everyone they need to read is *Endurance.* It's the inspiring story of Ernest Shackleton.

In 1914, this guy set out to do something no one had ever done before.

He wanted to cross Antarctica on foot.

That was the goal.
That was the mission.
And then life did what life does.
It changed the plan.

His ship, the *Endurance*, became trapped in ice and crushed beneath the surface.

It was gone.
In a single moment, his purpose flipped.

Yesterday's purpose was about achievement. Today's purpose became survival.

And here's what I love about Shackleton. He didn't throw a tantrum about how it was "supposed" to go. And he didn't cling to the plan he spent years building.

He made a new one.

"We will get home."

That became the mission.

For nearly a year and a half, he led 27 men across drifting ice, freezing water, and uncharted wilderness. And he didn't lose a single life.

Not one.

Why?

Because he faced the situation as it was, not as he hoped it would be. He asked one question over and over.

"Will this get my men home?"

That single line shaped every decision, every risk, and every ounce of morale they had left. Shackleton wasn't chasing glory anymore. He was fighting for something bigger than himself.

And this is the part every leader needs to remember.

You don't control the conditions.
You control the response.

When the conditions change, great leaders adapt with them.

They get honest.
They refocus.
They choose the purpose that matters *right now.*

If it doesn't push them toward their goal, they let it go. If it does, then they move, decisively, in that direction.

THE DIFFERENCE BETWEEN AN EXCUSE AND ALIGNMENT

Living a life with **NO EXCUSES** means living a life on purpose.

Purpose looks different for everyone. And it can change from day to day.

But when you decide what matters most **today,** and you take responsibility for acting in service of that decision, that's ownership.

Some days, that means getting up early, lacing up your shoes, and grinding long after everyone else has gone to bed.

Other days, it means slowing down, deleting half your calendar, and protecting your energy so you can show up tomorrow.

Both choices can be right.

Here's the difference.

When you say you're "too tired" to open a book but somehow have the energy to binge three episodes on Netflix, that's not fatigue.

That's avoidance. That's an excuse.

But when you skip reading because you genuinely need rest, turn the lights off early, and go to sleep?

That's alignment.

An excuse avoids responsibility. Alignment owns the choice and makes it on purpose.

Living with **NO EXCUSES** isn't about doing more. It's about being intentional and taking full responsibility for the direction of your life.

Every.
Single.
Day.

THE 1-1-1 WEEKLY FOCUS

Most people walk into a new week without a plan.

They react. They scramble. They run around putting out everyone else's fires and ignore their own. Then they look up on Friday, wondering why they feel overwhelmed, exhausted, and off track.

Here's the truth.

When you lack direction, stress piles up and excuses rush in to fill the gap. But when you start your week knowing exactly what matters, you start choosing the path you want to travel.

That's why the *1-1-1 Weekly Focus* works. It gives you clarity that simplifies your focus.

One word.
One priority.
One person.

That's it.

When your decisions are intentional, excuses are pushed away. And you move through your week with confidence instead of chaos.

Here's how it works.

1. ONE WORD

Your one word is your anchor. It's the direction you choose before the world tries to choose it for you.

Pick a word, any word, that matches the person you want to be this week.

Patient. Present. Confident. Energetic. Grateful. Still. Disciplined.

Write it down.
Say it out loud.
Let it set your emotional tone before anything else does.

This word becomes the voice in your head when distractions show up. It becomes the filter for what earns your time and what doesn't. It reminds you of the standard you chose, not the one life tries to hand you.

You don't need a 4-page checklist taped to your mirror. You need a simple target your brain can hit.

One word that reminds you,

"This is who I'm practicing being right now."

Once you know who you want to be, the next step is choosing what matters most.

2. ONE PRIORITY

Your one priority for this week is the thing that will matter a month from now. It's the thing that the *future you* will thank you for. It's the choice that actually moves your life forward instead of keeping you stuck in busywork.

Maybe it's strengthening a client relationship.
Showing up at your kid's game.
Or establishing a consistent bedtime.

It could be decluttering a space, rebuilding your workout routine, or creating a calmer morning so you don't start your day in panic mode.

The priority changes each week, but the rule doesn't.

Excuses show up when your priority is unclear. But when you name it, it shifts your state of mind. A clear priority puts you back in control of your time.

If it's not your priority, it doesn't get your prime energy. Period.

Now comes the part that makes the whole week meaningful.

3. ONE PERSON

Choosing one person to connect with each week expands your life.

Pick someone who inspires you, lifts your energy, or simply needs you. Then follow through.

Send the text to thank someone.
Make the call you "never have time for."
Grab lunch with a mentor.

Connection shifts your day. It brings meaning back into your week and reminds you that life isn't just about getting things done.

Life is about connecting as you go.

LIVE THE WEEK YOU WANT

Picture this.

It's Saturday night. You drop into bed after a long week. You exhale, and a small smile rises because you know you did it right. You stuck to your 1-1-1 and lived your life on purpose.

You lived your word. You honored your priority. You connected with someone.

You didn't do everything, but you did the things that mattered.

You said no when it protected your peace. And you said yes when it aligned with who you are becoming.

That is success.
That is alignment.
That is a week that counts.

YOUR LIFE ON PURPOSE

LIVING WITHOUT REGRETS

In 2014, my purpose finally aligned with who I wanted to become.

My purpose gave me clarity.
It strengthened my relationships.
It healed my mind.

When I look back on the Sochi Olympic Games, I don't regret a single sacrifice, hour, or moment it took to get there.

I feel a fierce sense of accomplishment in the work. I have great respect for my husband, who designed the sled I flew down the track on. Pride in being both a mother and an athlete. And deep gratitude for every person who supported me.

That season taught me something powerful.

When your purpose is clear and you move past your excuses, you become unstoppable.

SEE YOUR LIFE CLEARLY

Living without purpose is like stumbling through a dark room.

You move, but you keep hitting the same corners, stubbing the same toes, and making the same mistakes.

Purpose is the flashlight.

One click and suddenly you see what to say yes to, what to say no to, and what you can finally drop.

You see the habit you need to break.
The conversation you've avoided.
The project that actually matters.
The relationship that needs more of you and the one draining you dry.

Clarity doesn't erase challenges. It just makes the next right step obvious.

USE YOUR PURPOSE TO SHOW UP BETTER

Purpose strengthens your relationships because it strengthens *you.*

A 2022 study of more than 2,000 adults found that people with a clear sense of purpose didn't just stay in their relationships longer. They showed up better in them.

They were more present. More patient. More honest.

When you lead with your purpose, you listen instead of react. You repair instead of retreat. You stop keeping score and start building connection.

And here's the best part.

Relationships feel safer, deeper, and easier when you're aligned. Less tension. More laughter. More peace.

This is what purpose creates.

MEANING KEEPS YOU ALIVE

Viktor Frankl proved something most of us forget.

Purpose can hold your mind together, even when everything else is falling apart.

Inside the Nazi concentration camps, he watched people collapse under hopelessness while others survived because they had one thing left to hold on to.

Meaning.

Frankl made a choice.

He refused to let the camps define him.

He pictured finishing the book the Nazis destroyed. He pictured teaching again. He pictured helping people find meaning after the war.

That vision kept him alive.

His approach to therapy, known as logotherapy, rests on one truth. Your mind gets stronger the moment your life has purpose. And when it does, you truly begin to live.

LIVE ON PURPOSE TODAY

This chapter isn't about finding one perfect "why" and never questioning it again. It's about learning to realign in real time.

It's asking yourself, today, right now, what actually matters and then acting like it does.

When you live aligned, excuses don't stand a chance.

You know where to put your energy.
You spend less time debating and more time doing.
You recognize what deserves a yes and what requires a no.

You don't need a perfect plan to begin.
You just need a moment of honesty with yourself.

When you take time to determine what matters most each day, you start living on purpose, one aligned choice at a time.

CHAPTER 8

Mercy in the Middle

"Perfectionism tells you to quit. Compassion tells you to keep going."
—Jon Acuff

A MOMENT I CAN NEVER GET BACK

There's a story I've carried for years. And I still have to give myself mercy when I think about it.

It's not about a race I lost or a medal I missed. It's about a decision I didn't make. A moment I brushed off. And the consequence has followed me ever since.

Let me ask you something.

What's the moment you still carry?

The one you don't post about. The warning you ignored. The dream you shelved.

Which one still follows you?

It was the fall before the 2010 Olympics, and I was spending 3 long weeks at the Lake Placid Training Center.

One week down.

2 to go.

Athletes from all over the world packed into that building.

Bobsledders. Ski jumpers. Lugers. Speed skaters.

At breakfast you'd hear different languages bouncing off the walls while everyone waited for eggs and oatmeal. And even with all that variety, the routine got repetitive.

Wake up. Walk to the cafeteria. Eat.

Grab my gear. Load the team van. And drive 15 minutes through the trees to the track on the side of the mountain.

Then it was 3 hours of training.
Plyometrics. Sprints. Stretching. And my name would get called over the speakers.

I'd grab my sled. Sprint. Dive. Settle between the handles. And suddenly I was flying headfirst down a sheet of ice that didn't care who I was or what my goals were.

Cross the finish line. Climb into the truck. Ride to the top, and do it again.

When we finished sliding, we drove back to the training center where the repetition continued.

Unload sleds. Eat lunch. Work on equipment.
Hit the gym for 3 hours. Go to recovery. Eat dinner.
Call home. Fall into bed. Wake up and repeat.

That was my world.

The same day. Again. And Again.

And that's when it happened. Right in the middle of the most ordinary, forgettable moment of a forgettable day.

I was standing in the cafeteria line, staring at my banana and oatmeal, already counting the reps, sets, and sled rides that waited. And out of nowhere, a thought surfaced.

"I should call Michelle."

Michelle. My husband's cousin.

We'd see each other at a Christmas party or family reunion here and there. We weren't close, but she was always kind. Always playful with her nieces and nephews. And the second that thought hit, the excuses stormed in right behind it.

"Why would I call her? That'd be weird."

And honestly, if you've *never* called someone before, wouldn't it be weird?

Of course it would.
That's why the excuse felt so believable.

So, I let it go.

I went to the track. I slid. I focused on hundredths of a second like my life depended on it.

On the drive back to the Training Center the van rattled over potholes. The Adirondack wind pushed through the cracked windows.

And the thought came back.

Stronger this time.

"I should tell Michelle I'm thinking about her."

I hesitated.

And the excuses slipped right into the open space.

"What would I say? We're not even that close. I don't want it to be awkward."

All of that felt true. So, I shut it down again and went on with my day.

That night, I crawled into bed, pulled the scratchy training center blanket around me, and let my body finally relax.

And then it came again.

"Just call her."

I actually paused.
I thought about it.

I pictured picking up my phone, stepping out into the hallway and dialing her number. And for a second, I was right on the edge of action.

Then the excuses slid in. They were quiet and convincing.

"I'm too tired. I'll call her tomorrow." And I drifted off to sleep.

The next day, during lunch, my phone rang. It was my husband Janson. Before I could even say a word, he said one sentence that took the air out of my lungs.

"Michelle took her life last night."

I froze.
My thoughts. My breath. Everything in me just stopped.
I couldn't comprehend it.

And in that moment, I knew one thing for sure.

I'd felt the nudge.
I'd heard the whisper.
An opportunity opened.

And I'd excused myself out of it.

I'm not telling you this because I think I could've saved her.
I don't know what would've happened. None of us can know that.

I'm telling you because I know what it feels like to live with the question. To replay *"I'll call her tomorrow"* and wish I'd chosen differently.

For years, I carried that weight like a stone in my chest.

The guilt. The what-ifs. The imaginary conversations where I called and somehow everything changed.

Mercy reminded me that I'd done the best I knew how to do. It let me forgive myself, layer by layer. And if you've ever lived with regret, then you know exactly what I'm talking about.

And now, when I feel that quiet thought to reach out to someone, send the text, make the call, check on them, sit by them, or show up, I immediately move.

I don't wait for the perfect words or moment. And yes, I've had some very awkward conversations where people are wondering why I'm calling them.

But oh well.
I'm still glad I followed through.

I refuse to let an excuse talk me out of the simple things that make me a better human.

Ever again.

Mercy in the middle isn't weakness.

It's strength.

It lets you own the setback without collapsing under it. It teaches you to take immediate action the next time you feel that nudge.

Mercy keeps you pointed up when everything in you wants to spiral down. And it encourages you to keep moving forward.

You can't live a NO EXCUSES life without mercy.

Accountability without mercy turns into self-criticism.
Responsibility without mercy turns into pressure.
Growth without mercy becomes impossible.

This is why this chapter belongs in the middle of this book.

Because without mercy in the middle of our choices, **NO EXCUSES** would be harsh and impossible.

With mercy, NO EXCUSES becomes the most honest, human, and compassionate way to live.

HOW MERCY SHIFTS YOUR DIRECTION

What hit me after Janson's call wasn't just the heartbreak. It was the way I turned on myself.

I really believed that tearing myself down was the only way I would learn my lesson. But harsh thinking doesn't make you stronger. It just strips you of your confidence.

You've seen it.

Someone makes one mistake and decides that is who they are now.
So they pull back.
They play smaller.
They stop trying before anyone else can judge them.

Brené Brown says shame corrodes the part of us that believes we can change. And without mercy, your brain locks into a fixed mindset where every mistake feels final.

Mercy breaks the downward cycle. Mercy turns failure into feedback and lifts your slope upward again.

THE SLOPECHECK

Let me make this simple.

You are always heading somewhere.
Up toward ownership.
Or down into excuses.

When you graph a line, 2 things matter.

Where it starts.
And where it's headed.

On this graph, the intercept is you. Right now. In this moment

The SlopeCheck

Which direction are you heading?

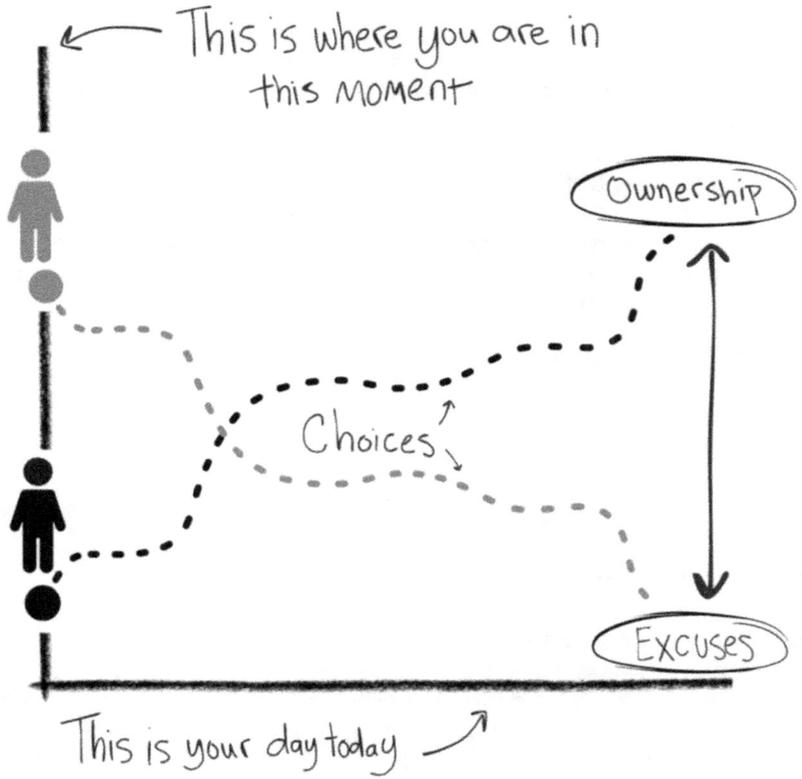

Some people start the day with support and stability. Others wake up much lower on the line because of stress, trauma, or circumstances they never chose.

Where you begin is real. But what happens from here comes down to your choices throughout the day.

You will rise into ownership.

Or you will slide into excuses.

So, let's do a quick SlopeCheck together.

Which direction are you heading *right now*?

Are your choices today moving you upward because you're in control of your emotions, being proactive, owning your outcomes, and following through?

Or are your choices drifting you downward because you're swimming in overwhelm, avoiding something, blaming the situation, or caught up in comparisons?

Your slope tells the truth.

And if you aren't sure how to get where you want to go, start by deciding where you want your line to end today. And then take one step to shift your slope in that direction.

A positive slope pulls you toward purpose. You show up, follow through, and do what needs to be done.

That's ownership.

Whereas a negative slope drags you down. You numb out, blame, or hide.

That's the path of excuses.

And this is where mercy steps in.

Mercy stops the free fall and turns your line upward again. It's the moment you interrupt the shame, forgive yourself, and choose differently. Mercy meets you exactly where you are and helps you redirect your day.

It doesn't matter where you start. What matters is where you choose to go next.

Your slope is your future, and you control the angle.

Without mercy, that slope drops fast. And no one proves that better than Samuel Langley.

MERCY WOULD HAVE MADE HIM FLY

Let me take you back to 1903.

There was one man everyone believed would conquer the sky.

Samuel Langley.

He had the money.
The experts
The government.
The prestige.

He had every advantage you could ask for. But when his aircraft crashed twice into the Potomac, everything inside him crashed too.

He expected perfection and he didn't give himself mercy.

He turned those failures into a story about not being good enough. He stopped trusting himself. And hesitation took over.

And because it wasn't perfect, he quit.

That's what a lack of mercy does.
It makes you question yourself instead of continuing forward.

So, 2 brothers in a bicycle shop beat him to the sky.

Langley started high on the slope with every resource in the world. The Wright brothers started low with nothing but grit and curiosity. And they kept getting back up.

After Langley's second crash, his slope didn't just dip. It nosedived.
He treated failure like the finish line instead of a pivot point.
But the Wright brothers did the opposite.

They faced every crash with mercy.
They let failure teach them.
And they refused to let it turn into a reason to quit.

Mercy lifted their slope and launched them straight into the history books.

But here's what I need you to understand.

You're either living like Langley.
Or you're living like the Wrights.

UPSLOPE IN 60 SECONDS

Mercy changes your slope in real time. So, let's check yours right now.

Get honest with yourself for a second.

NO EXCUSES.

Ask yourself, *"Is my slope pointing up or down right now?"*

Don't overthink it. Just answer.

Now finish this sentence.

"My slope is heading _________ because _____________."

Fill it in with whatever is true.

Your slope might be dropping today because of poor judgement.

Words you've said.
Time you've wasted.
Projects you're avoiding.

Maybe it feels flat, and you can't even tell if you're going up, down, or nowhere at all.

Or perhaps it's climbing because you finally followed through, served someone, or finished something you've been putting off for a while.

Whatever it is, say it out loud.

One sentence. One truth.

Next comes the UpSlope.

This is your chance to use one minute to take action and shift your slope upward.

When you're done reading this section, **set a timer for 60 seconds** and then make a one-degree shift.

Not a life overhaul. Just intentionally do something good.

Stand up. Move your body. Drink water. Clear the desk. Send the message. Shut the distraction down. Breathe like you mean it. Let go of what you can't control.

This part is up to you.

Take any small action that will UpSlope your line.

You don't rise by standing still.

Ready?

Start your 60 seconds and UpSlope.

...

...

...

...

...

...

This is how you reset your direction.

Especially on the days when everything goes wrong.

WHERE MERCY MATTERS MOST

There are 4 places in life where mercy matters most.

The tiny moments.
The people moments.
The moments you crash hard.
And the moments that change everything.

Let me show you.

THE TINY MOMENTS: THE BLANKET THIEF

It's 2 a.m.

You wake up freezing.

You reach over and realize the blanket is gone.
Not slightly shifted.
Gone.

Your spouse is wrapped in it like a human burrito, blissfully unaware that you are lying there with nothing but hope and a thin sheet.

For one dramatic second you consider yanking the blanket back with the full force of justice. But instead, you take a breath, tug a tiny corner your way, and let the rest go.

Because this is marriage.

Some nights you freeze, some nights you hog the covers, and forgiveness is what keeps you from keeping score.

Mercy is what turns a small irritation into a choice you don't regret.

THE PEOPLE MOMENTS

Mercy in the middle of the people moments are where forgiveness quietly changes everything. For you. And for others.

These are the moments when a mistake is made and shame wants to take over. When you disappoint yourself. Or when you say or do the wrong thing.

Mercy is what keeps you from quitting on yourself in those moments. It's the decision to stop punishing yourself. And instead, offer honesty with compassion.

When you forgive yourself, something settles.

Your body softens. Your mind quiets. You stop bracing for consequences that are no longer coming.

And when you extend that same mercy to others, you replace tension with the possibility to trust again. You choose repair over distance. And you loosen the grip the past has had on you.

Forgiveness doesn't excuse what hurt you.
It releases you from carrying it.

The people moments are where forgiveness quietly softens hearts. And if mercy matters in the quiet moments, it also matters when life gets loud.

THE HARD CRASHES: *"SO, ARE YOU GONNA QUIT?"*

The first time you try skeleton, you become acutely aware of the crashes waiting around every corner.

The pain.
The injuries.
The mental fatigue.
All of it.

After one insanely brutal practice, I sat bruised and bleeding on a wooden bench in the back of a freezing flatbed truck. I was riding up the mountain with athletes I didn't know.

I was giving a full verbal play-by-play of my misery when the athlete sitting directly across from me, his face hidden in the dark, leaned forward and said without sympathy,

*"Hey. In this sport, it's not **if** you crash but **when.** And when it happens, what are you gonna do? Quit?"*

He leaned back into the shadows.
I stopped complaining.
And that was the extent of our relationship.

His words were similar to those that my coach shared with me years earlier when I kept crashing in corner 12.

"It's not *if* you crash, but *when* you do, what will you *choose* to do next?"

We all hit walls throughout life.
Failure.
Grief.
Loneliness.

And the hardest crashes are the ones that unravel everything.

When addiction takes over. When you lose someone you love. When you are left holding the broken pieces and don't know where to begin.

You lose your job. Say something in anger. Or face a financial crisis you never saw coming.

But the real story isn't the fall.
It's what you do after the impact.

Without mercy, crashes become conclusions. But with it, mercy becomes the bridge between what happened in your life and how you choose to live next.

THE MOMENTS THAT CHANGE EVERYTHING

I was invited to speak at an event for cancer patients, and the second I walked into that room, the whole world seemed to pause.

You could feel the strength.
The faith.
The courage.

These were people who understood the value of a single minute in a way most of us never will.

It was extremely humbling.

After my talk, a woman named Lori came up to me. She had this grounded, unshakeable light about her.

A mom of 3 young kids.
Living with stage 4 breast cancer.
And still, she radiated more clarity than most of us on our best days.

I found myself wanting to understand the strength behind that peace, so I gently asked her what living with **NO EXCUSES** meant to her.

She didn't hesitate.

"It means remembering you have a choice every day. Choose to be happy. Choose to see the good. Choose gratitude. Let go of the past. Own your life. It all comes down to choice. Every. Single. Day."

THE ORIGAMI CRANE

Life is all about choices.

It's about what you choose to see or do during the moments that challenge you.

The small ones.
The painful ones.
And the ones that blindside you.

Mercy is the breath before the next move. It steadies your hands as you make adjustments.

I learned this on a snowy day in Nagano, Japan.

I was standing at the top of the track when an elderly man from the nearby town motioned me over with 2 fingers.

He held up a small square of purple paper, covered in bright flowers.

He pointed from the paper to me. Then he began to fold.

The man moved slowly and deliberately. A crease here. A correction there.

It took time.

He paused. He adjusted. He tried again.
I could tell he cared about getting it just right.

I watched him shape the paper into a beautiful origami crane. When he finished, he lifted it with a proud smile. We didn't share a language, but I knew exactly what he was saying.

He took pride in that moment, in that creation, and in offering something meaningful.

I smiled back and bowed in gratitude as he placed the crane in my hands.

I still have it today. It's a small, colorful reminder that beauty is built one tiny, merciful adjustment at a time.

GIVE YOURSELF PERMISSION

When you slow down long enough to listen, you realize something most people miss.

Excuses aren't flaws.
They're just signals.

When you make an excuse, what you're really asking from yourself is permission.

Permission to move forward.
Permission to rest.
Permission to try again without punishing yourself first.

So, let's dig through the layers of your "go-to excuse" and figure out what's underneath it all. We're going to Mercy Map this together.

But before we do, let me show you how this plays out in my life.

NOELLE'S MERCY MAP

1. **My go-to excuse is "I'm too busy."**
   That excuse costs me my health and my sanity.

2. **Underneath it is overwhelm.**

3. **Under the overwhelm is the fear that I am not doing enough.**

4. **And under that fear is the belief that if I slow down for even a second, everything will fall apart.**

5. **What I actually need is permission.**
   Permission to rest.
   Permission to sit still.
   Permission to do nothing and not feel guilty about it.

So, I took a nap this week.
It was harder than it should have been.
And it was incredible.

Naming the layers stripped the shame off the excuse.

That's what mercy does. It lets you respond to what you need instead of punishing yourself for having limits.

That's what I want for you.

THE MERCY MAP

A 5-step exercise to uncover the truth under your excuses

Alright. Let's do this together. Grab a pen.

Step 1: Name Your Go-To Excuse and What it Costs You

Everyone has a signature excuse. The one that shows up fast.

"I'm too tired."
"I don't have time."
"It wasn't my fault."
"I'm not ready yet."
"I'll just do it myself."

Pick yours. Write it down. No sugarcoating.

Now write the cost.

Does it cost you sleep?
Peace?
Integrity?
Your health?
Your goals?

Naming the excuse and the cost immediately weakens its grip.

Step 2: Name the Real Feeling

This matters, so hear me clearly. It is okay to feel this way.

Under every excuse is a feeling you would rather avoid.
Overwhelm. Embarrassment. Fear. Exhaustion. Uncertainty.

Your brain isn't broken. It's signaling you.

Name the feeling. Write it down.

Step 3: Name the Fear Driving It

This is the step most people skip because fear likes to hide.

Every excuse is protecting a fear.

Fear of failing.
Fear of disappointing someone.
Fear of being judged.
Fear of losing control.
Fear of starting and not finishing.

What fear is driving yours? Write it down.

Step 4: Call Out the Belief Behind it

This is the moment things get real.

Under the fear is a belief that has been quietly steering your choices.

It sounds like this.

"People will judge me if they see the real me."
"I can't let anyone down."
"If I slow down, something bad will happen."
"People expect perfection."
"It's all on me."

Name the belief. Put it on paper.

Step 5: Give Yourself Permission

Now write the permission you *actually* need.

Use this sentence.

"What I really need is permission to _________, so I will _________."

Here are a few examples:

What I really need is permission to be honest, so I will say how I actually feel.

What I really need is permission to let go, so I will stop gripping the outcome.

What I really need is permission to say no, so I will decline what is draining me.

This is mercy in motion.

Now take one small step that matches it.
Just one.

If you did this exercise, then you felt the shift.

You saw the fear and belief hiding underneath an excuse that has been running your life. And you are allowing mercy to map out your next move.

Now let's zoom out.

A LIFE BUILT ON MERCY

THE RESET ROCK

Some days requires a complete reset.

Years ago, I was having one of "those days."

You know what I'm talking about.

A day when everything feels off and you feel stretched thin, like a rubber band that has already snapped once.

So, I walked into my backyard, picked up a smooth rock and did something really simple.

I drew a red circle on it. Then I wrote one word across the front in bold black letters.

RESET.

I closed my eyes, took a slow breath, and pressed that circle like it was a button.
It obviously didn't do anything on the outside. But inside of me, that moment gave me permission to begin again.

To have a better day.
To move forward.
A fresh start.

That rock still sits on my desk because sometimes I just need to remind myself to reset. Look at where I am on my slope. And do one small thing to move myself in the direction that I want to go.

LEADING WITH MERCY

Leadership isn't about powering through when things are off and your team is stretched thin.

Real leadership is knowing when to hit the reset button.

When to pause.
When to slow down.
When to adjust instead of push harder.

The strongest leaders use mercy as a tool.

They practice mercy and create trust. They grow relationships. And they earn influence that comes from authenticity.

Leaders who live with mercy reflect without judgment. They adjust without spiraling, offer grace without enabling, and rest without quitting.

And because they reset themselves, they give the people they lead permission to make corrections and reset too.

KAIZEN: ONE SMALL CORRECTION AT A TIME

There's a word in Japanese that has changed the way I think about growth.

The word is **Kaizen.**

It means continuous improvement through small, deliberate corrections.

One choice.
One adjustment.
One moment of awareness at a time.

I watched the elderly craftsman fold that origami crane with a level of attention I'd never seen.

His hands moved slowly and intentionally. When something drifted, he corrected it immediately.

No shame. No frustration. **NO EXCUSES.**

Just awareness and adjustment.

That's Kaizen.
That's mercy.
And that's how real transformation happens.

THE ONE-DEGREE SHIFT

The Mercy Map isn't about filling out a worksheet. It was about naming the truth and shifting your slope upward just one degree at a time.

When you acknowledge an excuse, that's one degree.
When you name the emotion, another degree.
The fear? One more.
The belief? Another.

And when you give yourself permission to take action, a big shift happens. You UpSlope and your line drives toward ownership.

Mercy is the difference between learning from life's experiences and losing yourself in the mess of it all.

WHAT MERCY MAKES POSSIBLE

A life with mercy becomes a life where you can live without fear.

Because mercy keeps you honest without being harsh.
It keeps you moving without shame.
It keeps your slope pointed up, even on the days you slip.

When you live with mercy in the middle, excuses fade and everything changes.

Your choices get sharper.
Relationships get stronger.
Leadership gets deeper.

Your confidence grows and resilience multiplies.

And you stop spiraling because you know you can hit the reset button and have a fresh start.

Mercy gives you permission to fail and to rise again and again.

And when you rise with mercy in the middle, you always have the next 60 seconds to begin again.

CHAPTER 9

Build Consistent Results

"Preparation is what makes consistency possible."
—*Bill Walsh*

ONE FOOT IN FRONT OF THE OTHER

When the 2010 Olympic team was announced and my name was on the list, it should have been the best moment of my life.

Music.
Laughter.
Energy.
Everyone hugging. Everyone cheering.

I had made it. I was finally an Olympian.

But the second I realized it, panic took the wheel and every warning light on the dashboard came on at once.

I was in the foyer of the Laudinella Hotel in St. Moritz, Switzerland, surrounded by teammates who were celebrating. And I was sitting on a hotel couch, having an internal meltdown as I thought about the pressure of the Games.

I pictured the camera crews. The interviews. And the icy corners that I didn't understand. The speed of my competitors My family's logistics. And my coach's expectations.

The crowd cheering.
The reporters waiting.
And the world watching.

And underneath all of it, there was a voice screaming in my head.

I don't know if I can do this.

Fear spread through me like a wildfire in a desert forest. So, I scanned the foyer for an answer.

Then I saw him.
Coach Brian Shimer.
5-time Olympian in bobsledding.

He was sitting in a corner by himself. He looked steady and calm while the room spun in celebration.

I desperately needed that calm. So, I walked toward him, doing that awkward half-smile thing you use when you're trying to look fine even though you are absolutely not fine. Well, he saw right through it and motioned for me to sit down. And without taking a breath, I unloaded everything.

How do you make it count?
How do you stay focused?
How do you manage everyone's expectations?

I feel so much pressure!

I was filled with every excuse imaginable.

I wanted to please everyone. I doubted my ability. I justified my emotions as normal for a rookie. I blamed my inexperience. And I avoided the truth.

Eventually, I paused long enough for him to raise his eyebrows, smile, and give me a look that said, *Are you finished?*

I took a deep breath and held it. I was waiting for him to tell me the Olympic secret to success. Instead, he tilted his head, paused, and said this.

"Let me ask you a question, Noelle. If I put a 2-foot board on the ground and asked you to walk across it, could you do it?"

He held up his hands, measuring the space like he was showing off a 2-foot fish.

I nodded, even though my face said, *"What does this have to do with the Olympics?"*

"Okay," he said. *"Could you jog across it?"*

"Ya," I responded.

"Could you sprint across it?" He quickly replied.

I had run track my entire life. I imagined a narrow lane beneath my feet.

"Of course," I said.

Then Coach Shimer leaned in and his eyes narrowed.

"Now imagine that same board is 1,000 feet in the air." He pointed up as though it was really there. *"Really imagine it."*

He paused long enough for the picture to sink in. Then he calmly asked,

"Could you walk across it?"

My mind transported straight to the edge of the Grand Canyon. The board stretched from one cliff to the other and a thin, sharp wind brushed past my face.

"No," I said, slowly shaking my head.

He nodded. Like he already knew how I would respond.

"Could you jog across it?"

I pictured a river 1,000 feet below me, carving through the canyon floor like a tiny silver thread. There was absolutely no way I'd walk across that thing.

So, I shook my head.

"Okay. Could you sprint across it?" He asked. *"Could you run as fast as you possibly could from one end to the other?"*

If I *had* to cross that board, I would be on my hands and knees praying to every angel assigned to me.

"No," I said. "I couldn't."

"Why not?" he quickly asked. Pointing a finger at me like a school teacher calling on a student.

I thought for a second and responded.

"Because I'd be afraid to fall."

A slight smile crossed his face. *"Exactly,"* he said. *"You'd be afraid to fall."*

He let that sit for a second. Then he continued.

"That board never changed. Only the environment did. You're so focused on the distractions around you that you've forgotten that it has been, and always will be, about placing one foot in front of the other and focusing on where you want to go, rather than where you don't want to end up. Don't quit on yourself before you get there."

I was trying to process this analogy and understand what it meant exactly. So, when I didn't respond right away, he leaned in closer and continued.

"Noelle, when you get to the Olympics, there will be distractions everywhere. Cameras. Crowds. Pressure. Noise. You need to prepare for that. Then, once you're there, keep it simple. You're an Olympian now. Just focus on the small things that will actually get you across the finish line."

It immediately clicked.

Prepare for the challenges. Control what you can control. Focus on your goal and don't quit.

Just take one small step. Then the next.

Two weeks later, when I walked into the Opening Ceremonies in Vancouver, Canada with Team USA, I remembered exactly who I was.

I'm an Olympian.

Olympians aren't made at the Olympics. Olympians are made in the tiny, countless, consistent choices no one sees.

I was proud to be among those who were striving to be their absolute best day after day. Rep after rep. And choice after choice.

I knew that each of us understood something the world frequently forgets.

You don't win by avoiding the distractions.
You win by preparing for them.
And then taking one small step after another.

THE POWER OF LITTLE THINGS

Let me tell you something you probably don't want to hear.

Your life doesn't fall apart because of one big failure. It drifts because of the tiny things you don't prepare for. The ones that don't seem to matter.

Here's the truth.

One small step in the right direction can move you closer to everything you want. And one small step in the wrong direction can quietly pull you down even faster.

Because time doesn't care which direction you're headed. It just multiplies whatever you keep doing.

That's why the little things always win.

Let me show you what I mean.

PREPARE FOR THE STORMS

The Golden Gate Bridge is one of the most photographed structures on the planet. It's iconic. Majestic. A marvel of engineering.

But here's the part nobody posts on Instagram.

Workers paint that bridge. Every. Single. Day.

Not because it looks dirty.
Not because it's falling apart.

But because if they ever stop preparing for the stormy weather, corrosion would take hold and the bridge would slowly lose its strength.

Now imagine this.

The crew decides to take a break. Not forever. Just for a little while. And then a few days turn into a few weeks.

Nothing changes at first.

Cars still cross. Tourists still snap photos. The bridge still *looks* strong. But underneath the surface, metal starts to weaken. Tiny cracks form. Rust creeps in quietly.

And then one day, a storm rolls through and the bridge falls apart.

You've been here.

You skip one disciplined decision. And then another. Until one night you find yourself standing in the kitchen at 9 p.m. eating peanut butter out of the jar, wondering how your life got so off track.

The storm doesn't create the weakness. It exposes what wasn't maintained.

That's how your life works too.

Skipping one workout doesn't ruin your health.
Leaving one dish in the sink doesn't wreck your marriage.
Letting one routine s ide doesn't destroy your confidence.

But over time?

Strength leaks.
Trust erodes.
Stability thins.

And when pressure hits, the things you assumed would hold you together suddenly don't. Not because you failed. But because you stopped taking the small steps forward.

ONE SMALL THING CAN STOP EVERYTHING

The small details are critical.
The right ones move you forward. And the wrong ones ground you.

In July of 2024, Delta Air Lines came to a grinding halt.

No weather disaster.
No pilot strike.
No mechanical failure.

Just one little software update.
That's it.

A single line of code brought down the entire system. And the team was unprepared.

Hundreds of thousands of passengers were stranded. Computers crashed. Flights stopped. Screens went black. Planes sat motionless on tarmacs for hours and families slept on airport floors.

The cost?
Over $500 million. And years of trust undone in a day.

Delta's CEO called it a wake-up call.
And he was right.

And this is exactly how it happens in your life.

One habit you don't fix.
One decision you keep delaying.
One routine you quietly skip.

At first, it's just a glitch. It's annoying, but manageable. Until one day, everything crashes and you're wondering what just happened.

THE TOUCH OF A DOMINO

There's a physics fact I love.

A simple touch of a domino can knock over another domino that's 1.5 times bigger than itself. That doesn't sound impressive until you keep going.

This means that if you start with one domino, and the next one is a little bigger, then a little bigger, by the 18th you've built enough force to knock over a building.

By the 23rd, the Eiffel Tower.
By the 31st, the stack reaches the moon.

This is cause and effect. Small actions don't stay small. They compound. They grow.

So, let's bring this back to your day.

You make your bed. That's domino one.
You open your budgeting app for 60 seconds. Another domino.
You apologize first. Drink a glass of water. Or you might just read one sentence from a book you've been ignoring.
Not a chapter. Calm down.

Each small win tips the next one. And suddenly, like a domino reaching the moon, your actions take you places you never knew were possible.

And when you simplify the steps, you're more likely to repeat them.

YOU'RE DOING TOO MUCH

Let me tell you something I learned the hard way.

When I was a rookie athlete, I tried to fix everything at once.
Corner 4. Corner 9. Corner 10. My start. My form. My breathing.
Basically, all of it.

I wanted the domino to hit the moon on the first try. But it was way too much to focus on a hundred goals at once. So, my motivation collapsed and I didn't get anywhere.

You know what I'm talking about.

New Year's hits.

You buy the gym membership. You go every day. For 3 hours. But then 4 weeks later, you're exhausted, discouraged, and Googling, *"Why am I sore all the time?"*

So, you quit. Again.

And you promise yourself you'll try again next January, like that's part of the training plan.

Well, you're not alone.

That's because the human brain can't handle massive overhauls. It thrives on clarity and focus. It needs to know exactly what to do and when to do it. And it needs a simple plan.

DECIDE BEFORE THE MOMENT

Researchers found something simple and powerful. People who use *"If this happens, **then** I'll do that"* plans are 3 times more likely to follow through.

Why?
Because the decision is already made.

No debating with yourself.
No dramatic inner monologue.
You just move.

It looks like this:

If the alarm rings, **then** I get up.
If I open the fridge at night, **then** I grab water first.

That's it.

If you want a different life, stop hoping you'll feel motivated. Hope is not a strategy. Decide your response before the moment shows up. **NO EXCUSES.**

When you know what you want in life, preparation becomes mandatory. You don't leave it to chance. You get ready on purpose.

And your purpose is always guided by who you say you want to become.

PEOPLE LIKE US DO THINGS LIKE THIS

When you decide who you are, you start acting like that person.

Here's what I mean.

Researchers at Stanford ran a simple study with preschoolers.

Yes. Preschoolers.

They created a mess in a classroom. Then they split the kids into two groups.

One group was asked,

"Can you help clean this up?"

The other group was told,

"You are helpers. Helpers clean things up."

Same kids.
Same mess.
Completely different behavior.

The kids who were asked to *help* pitched in briefly.
The kids who were told they *were helpers* stepped in faster, stayed longer, and took ownership.

Why?

Because when behavior is tied to identity, effort stops feeling optional.

They weren't deciding *what to do.*
They were acting like *who they were.*

This effect isn't limited to preschoolers. A similar study in London reframed public transit drivers as *"active people who look for chances to move."*

No workout plan. No incentives. Just identity.

And it's no surprise what happened next.

Drivers started walking more. Stretching more. Taking the stairs.
They didn't *try* to be active.
They behaved like active people.

And nobody understands identity-driven action better than the U.S. Marines.

"Marines don't hesitate. Marines take action."

They don't debate.
They don't negotiate.
They don't ask how they *feel* first.

And this matters. Because identity tells your brain one powerful sentence:

"People like us do things like this."

And once that sentence is installed, you take action and move past your excuses.

POWER IN THE PAUSE

So, pause for a minute.

What kind of person do you want to become?

Someone who helps others?
Someone who keeps promises?
Someone who doesn't hesitate?

When you know who you want to become, everything becomes clearer. Decisions get simpler. Self-doubt gets quieter. And you stop negotiating with yourself because you already know what kind of person you're choosing to be.

Identity alone doesn't always carry you through the daily grind.

Even when you know who you are, there will be days you feel stuck. Days you don't know the next right move. Days where improvement feels out of reach.

In those moments, preparation fills the gap between who you are and what to do next. And preparation doesn't look like pushing harder. It looks like pausing long enough to reflect on what just happened and on how you want to move forward.

That pause creates clarity. And when you do this consistently, your results begin to change.

YOU'LL WANT TO MAKE TIME FOR THIS

During his first year as an assistant coach for Brigham Young University's Women's Basketball team, Lee Cummard reached out to me. He wanted to help his team level up.

That alone tells you a lot about him.
He's humble. He's curious.
And he's the kind of person who is always chasing improvement.

Here's what I told him.

Hand every athlete a journal. At the end of every practice and game, give them one minute to pause and reflect on **The Daily 3** questions.

1. **What went well today?**

2. **What didn't go so well today?**
3. **How will I choose to improve tomorrow?**

That's it.
One minute.
60 seconds of ownership.

Coach Cummard saw the value immediately.

Today, he's BYU's head coach and one of the best in the nation because he reflects before he reacts and prepares before he proceeds. And he teaches his team to do the same.

Now here's the contrast.

About a week later, a high school football coach from southern Utah reached out.

They had talent.
They had resources.
But their results were terrible.

I gave him the same advice.

Pause. Reflect. Use The Daily 3.

His response?

"We don't have time for that. We're pushing ourselves to the end of every practice as it is."

Seriously?
You don't have 60 seconds to get better?

Got it.
Mystery solved.

If you never stop to look at what's working and what isn't, you won't improve.
You just repeat the same season. The same mistakes. The same results and the same frustration.

The Daily 3 needs to be a non-negotiable in sales, leadership, parenting, athletics, and any part of life where getting better actually matters.

It clears your mind so that your body can move in the right direction.

And if you feel stuck, inconsistent, or like progress keeps slipping away, here's the good news.

Nothing is wrong with you.

It just means one of the Excusers has taken the wheel. And once you spot it, you can put yourself back in the driver's seat.

WHO'S ACTUALLY DRIVING?

You already met the 5 Excusers back in Chapter 2, and they haven't gone anywhere. But listen up.

The moment you reach for consistency, they rush to the front of your car.

If you want to improve any area in your life, you have to stay in the driver's seat. Because the second you stop preparing for the road ahead, one of the **5 Excusers** takes the wheel.

The Blamer swears you'd already be there if the road weren't so unfair. Too many turns. Too many detours. Too many people in your way.

The Avoider tells you not to start the car yet. Tomorrow feels like a better driving day. Or maybe after you wash all the windows. Again.

The Justifier talks you into pulling over. You've earned a break. The empty parking lot where nothing's happening is fine. You'll get back on the road later.

The Doubter reminds you of the last time you tried this route and stalled out halfway there. And who knows, the gas pedal might quit again. Best not to push it.

The Pleaser changes the destination so everyone else is happy. And suddenly you're wedged in the back of a 12-passenger van, nodding politely while your own goal disappears in the rearview mirror.

The 5 Excusers show up fast and they'll talk you out of every good thing you're trying to do.

But listen, *they* are not *you*.
They're just patterns you've practiced and moments you weren't ready for.

So, check in with yourself for a second.

Who's actually behind the wheel of your life right now?

You?
Or one of the 5 Excusers?

If you want to drive your life toward your dream destination, you need a system stronger than your excuses.

And here it is.

THE NO EXCUSES METHOD

The **NO EXCUSES Method** is how you prepare in advance so you stay consistent when motivation drops and pressure hits.

You've already learned these tools in earlier chapters. But this is where they work together.

3 steps.
3 tools.
One minute each day.

This is how you prepare to take the next step when the ground feels a thousand feet in the air.

Step 1: Decide who you are.
Step 2: Keep it simple every week.
Step 3: Own it every day.

It isn't about pushing harder.
It's about preparing smarter.

Step 1: Decide Who You Are
Tool: The Sentence You Don't Argue With

> If you want to kick the Excusers out of your car, this is where you
> start.
>
> Consistency doesn't begin with more effort. It begins with a decision.
>
> Consistency doesn't begin with more effort. It begins with a decision.
> This decision.

Who are you?

Just like the preschoolers in the Stanford study. The kids who were told they were "helpers" stepped up and stayed engaged. While the kids who were simply asked to help lost interest and walked away.

When you've already decided who you are, the next step becomes obvious. Even on hard days. You stop debating. You stop procrastinating. And you do the thing your brain wants to avoid.

Here's what this looks like.

The Weekly **Sentence You Don't Argue With** is exactly what it sounds like.

You decide who you are each week so you don't negotiate with yourself when things get hard.

For example, instead of asking,
"Do I feel like doing this today?"

You already decided:
"I'm someone who follows through."

So, when the alarm goes off, you get up.
When the workout feels optional, you move anyway.
When the conversation feels uncomfortable, you have it.

Because this is *who* you *are*.

Now make it yours.

Create your **Sentence You Don't Argue With.**

"I'm someone who________________________."

Not who you hope to be.
But who you are choosing to be.

This is the one I constantly come back to: *"I'm someone who doesn't make excuses."*

When I choose this sentence, I finish what I start, treat people better, and make cleaner decisions all week long.

Take one minute to decide who you are becoming each week.

Step 2: Keep It Simple Every Week
Tool: The 1-1-1 Weekly Focus

Most people don't lose consistency because life gets hard. They lose it because life gets crowded.

Too many priorities.
Too many directions.
Too much noise.

So, we simplify it.

Pick one day each week to do the **1-1-1 Weekly Focus.**

One word.
One priority.
One person.

Here's how it works.

Choose **one word,** any word, that matches the person you want to be this week.

Patient. Present. Confident. Energetic. Grateful. Still. Disciplined.

Then, narrow down **one priority** for this week. The one thing that will still matter a month from now.

Finally, pick **one person**. Someone who inspires you, lifts your energy, or simply needs you. Then follow through and connect with them.

Consistency doesn't require doing more. It requires deciding ahead of time what deserves your attention.

This is how you prepare your focus before the week tries to steal it. It gives your effort a direction to drive towards when distractions show up. And it keeps your eyes focused on where you want to go, rather than where you don't want to end up.

Step 3: Own It Every Day
Tool: The Daily 3

This is where preparation becomes personal. And this is where mercy belongs in the middle.

Because no matter how well you plan, some days will still be hard. And some days you'll still fall short.

The **Daily 3** is a 60-second pause that prepares you to adjust instead of spiral.

I like to do this step each night before bed.

But just pick a consistent time each day to answer 3 simple questions.

1.   **What went well today?**

2.   **What didn't go so well today?**

3.   **How will I choose to improve tomorrow?**

This isn't about judgment.
It's about ownership.

You prepare for tomorrow by telling the truth today. You course-correct early, before one day off turns into a week or a month you regret.

DON'T LOOK DOWN

When Coach Shimer told me to focus on placing one foot in front of the other, he wasn't telling me the Olympics would be easy. He was telling me to remember who I was, to prepare for the distractions and let go of the things I couldn't control.

He was telling me to expect the height.
To expect the pressure.
To expect the fear.
And to take a step anyway.

That's the **NO EXCUSES Method.**

Step 1: Decide who you are.
Step 2: Keep it simple every week.
Step 3: Own it every day.

You don't move forward by staring at how far you could fall. You move forward by deciding who you are, preparing for what's coming, and choosing to take the next step forward.

PREPARATION IS THE KEY TO CONSISTENCY. PERIOD.

One of the strongest examples of preparation leading to consistency comes from Toyota.

On their production floors, any employee can pull the Andon cord and stop the entire assembly line the moment something looks off. When that cord is pulled, progress stalls.

You know this feeling.

You miss a mortgage payment because the furnace needed repairs.
You miss a workout because the flu hit hard.
Or you fall back into an old habit and suddenly your momentum stops.

But just like Toyota, the stall doesn't last long when you're prepared for it.

Their workers know exactly what the issue means and how to move into immediate correction. They fix the problem fast so the line gets back on track with as little lost progress as possible.

The same principle applies to you.

Setbacks will surface. Slip ups will happen. Expect resistance and delays.

Your job is to recognize the moment it happens, correct it quickly, and get yourself moving forward again.

Don't let one slip turn into two.
Don't let two turn into a week.
Reset fast. Get back in motion. And keep going.

OWN YOUR BEDTIME ROUTINE

One of the simplest places to create a day filled with consistent habits is by preparing the night before. But remember, simple doesn't mean easy.

Nighttime is when your willpower drops, your excuses get loud, and one more episode of "resting" turns into hours.

You tell yourself you're winding down.
Your Excusers call it 'self-care.'

I fall into this trap too.

But staying up needlessly late isn't resting. It's an Excuser stealing energy from tomorrow.

Research shows that regular sleep schedules strengthen the brain's ability to focus, learn, and recover. Which explains why everything feels harder when you're running on fumes.

So, kick that Excuser out of your bedtime routine.

Take 60 seconds and ask yourself the Daily 3.

"What's one thing I can prepare tonight that will make tomorrow easier?"

Set a screen curfew. Put your phone in another room and shut things down earlier than you want to. Then, listen to soft music or grab a book.

Your night sets the tone.
Your morning sets the pace.
When you prepare both on purpose, you eliminate half the excuses before the day even starts.

FOCUS ON WHERE YOU WANT TO GO

When I walked into the Opening Ceremonies in Vancouver, Canada, in 2010, I felt the joy that only comes after years of grinding for a moment. But when it was time to compete, I didn't rely on motivation.

I relied on my preparation.

My coach told me to be prepared for the distractions, pressure, and doubt that would hit me every single day.

Then he said, *"Place one foot in front of the other and focus on where you want to go."*

But that advice only works when you have a plan for how to move through it.
Otherwise, fear decides where your focus goes.

Preparation is what steadies you when the pressure hits. It's the thing that keeps your feet moving when your fear wants you to stop.

Preparation beats motivation every time.

LIVE THE LIFE YOU WANT. CONSISTENTLY.

Consistency isn't an accident.

It's who you decide to be. The simple plan you choose. And the tiny actions you repeat when no one's watching.

It's one foot in front of the other.

One word.
One priority.
One person at a time.

A consistent life shows up when you pause long enough to reflect on your day and then choose how you will improve tomorrow.

This is how progress compounds. This is how winning cultures are made. This is how you get the results you want.

Don't quit on yourself before you get there.

Choose to live the NO EXCUSES life.

CHAPTER 10

1% Better

"If you shrink the behavior small enough,
success becomes inevitable."
—*B.J. Fogg*

SIMPLE ISN'T EASY

Becoming an Olympian is VERY simple.
It only requires one thing, but most people won't do it.

Ready for the secret?
Here it is.

Be 1% better today.

That's it.

Then you do it again tomorrow.
And the next day.
And the next thousand days.

See? Simple.

But here's the catch. Simple isn't the same as easy.

Simple is savage.

Simple means sacrificing comfort, sleep, convenience, ego, and every excuse you've ever used to protect yourself. You hand it all over. Willingly.

The reason most people don't become Olympians is because 1% is just too much to ask.

To get to the top, you don't just train. You trade.

Piece by piece, you trade who you are for who you're trying to become.

It isn't reserved for the lucky or gifted. It's for the people willing to show up for the smallest improvement, over and over and over again.

THE GRIND NO ONE SEES

Every day leading up to the 2010 Olympic Games, I gave it everything I had. And I don't mean the cute, inspirational-poster version of "everything." I mean the kind that rearranges your life, your priorities, and honestly, pieces of your soul.

Early alarms. Sprint sessions. Heavy lifts. Torn calluses. Freezing cold. Bruised hips.

Years of training for 5 seconds of sprinting, diving onto my stomach and flying headfirst down a mile of ice at freeway speeds.

And every day, I made the same simple choice.

Be 1% better today than yesterday.

And over time, it all added up.

WHEN ENCOURAGEMENT MISSES THE MARK

The morning of my Olympic competition in Vancouver, Canada, I felt every emotion possible.

Stress. Joy. Fear. Peace. All of it.

In a few hours, I'd be racing and the world would be watching.

I was finally an Olympian.

After breakfast, I headed back to my dorm room in the Olympic Village. I pulled my key card from my back pocket, ready to swipe the lock, when 2 voices called out from down the hall.

"Hey, good luck, Noelle! We'll be cheering for you. You've got this!"

2 bobsledders leaned against the wall. Grinning like proud siblings. We'd been traveling the world together for years and their confidence in me lifted something inside my chest.

I smiled. Because right then, I knew I belonged there. I felt that anything was possible.

My hand closed around the doorknob when one of them shouted, *"Oh, by the way!"*

I leaned back into the hallway. They exchanged a look and yelled something I'll never forget.

"Whatever you do, do not finish fourth! You can finish fifth or tenth or even dead last. But fourth is the worst place. You get nothing. Gold, silver, bronze, then nothing. Good luck!"

They gave me a thumbs-up like they'd just reminded me to pack an umbrella. And then they walked away.

Fourth.

The place no one remembers.

Good to know.

I shook it off and walked into my room.

4 RUNS. ONE TRUTH.

That evening moved faster than I could process. It was a blur of adrenaline, excitement, doubt, and the strange relief of finally competing in the race I'd trained years for.

At the Olympics, skeleton isn't a one-run event. It's 4 trips down a mile-long track.

Every run counts.

None can be dropped.

There are no do-overs. No second chances.

When you cross the finish line, all 4 runs are combined and the clock reveals the truth.

As I stood at the top for my final run, I could feel every sacrifice pressing into this moment. My husband and 2-year-old daughter were at the bottom. All of my family stood in the cold, cheering for me. Believing in me.

The green light illuminated and I sprinted with everything I had. My spikes pushed through the ice. My heart pounded. Then I dove onto my sled and the world narrowed into the 1% actions and processes that I had accumulated over the years.

Corner 1 to corner 2.
Eyes down, eyes up.
Exhale. Relax the hand.
Drive. Blink. Steer. Breathe.

Every cue fired in perfect sequence.

My body executed what my brain had rehearsed thousands of times.

The finish line approached and I stretched my helmet forward to cross it.

When I pushed up off my sled to see my ranking, my stomach dropped.

Fourth place.

I missed an Olympic medal by 0.1 of a second.

I was so painfully close to the podium.

The bobsledders were right. Fourth place really is the worst.

TINY THINGS. HUGE CONSEQUENCES.

I retired after that race without an announcement. I simply walked away. Home mattered more to me than sliding and it was time to close that chapter.

But months later, a thought kept coming back.

Why did I finish a tenth of a second off the podium?

I finally sat down, opened the footage, and forced myself to watch my Olympic race frame by frame.

My lines matched the medalists. The steers matched. The speeds identical.

Then I saw it.

I stopped the video and leaned in.
You've got to be kidding me.

My shoelaces.

I was the only athlete in medal contention wearing spikes with exposed shoelaces.

Every top competitor had theirs sealed under zippers or tucked beneath fitted velcro straps. My laces were in the open and causing the tongue of my shoes to catch air like tiny parachutes.

Everyone had *always* worn shoes with exposed shoelaces in the past. But they had evolved, and I hadn't.

My stomach sank.

How did I miss something so small and simple?

I took screenshots of my shoes and the medalists and sent them to my coach.

"Could this have cost me 0.1 of a second?"

His response came instantly.

"Oh man, Noelle. That would do it."

We test equipment in wind tunnels and study friction and drag. Every microsecond matters. And the laws of physics don't make exceptions.

It was determined that the exposed laces cost me precious time because of aerodynamic drag. At *least* a tenth of a second. And that's the margin I lost by.

I missed an Olympic medal because of my shoelaces!

Did you catch that?

Read it again. Just so you can feel my pain.

I missed an *Olympic medal* because of my *shoelaces.*

Here's a fun fact, though. I've got the highest Olympic finish of any skeleton athlete since 2010, male or female, who dared to race with exposed shoelaces.

Where's my medal for that one, huh?

THE LESSON HIDDEN IN A SHOELACE

My runs weren't perfect in the 2010 Games, and there were other areas that would have benefitted from a marginal improvement, but the fact remains.

After reaching speeds of 90 miles per hour and traveling nearly 6000 meters on ice, it wasn't a big mistake that cost me greatly. It was the smallest detail.

Here's the point.

The small things decide big outcomes.

The little things you do, or don't do... they matter.

Sometimes the breakthrough is hiding in a shoelace. But usually, in our lives, it's found in a habit or a tiny blind spot.

When you start noticing the small and simple things in your life and then choose to get 1% better each day, over time, you'll create massive success for yourself.

WANT BIG CHANGE? START SMALL

For years, British Cycling was painfully average. So average that top bicycle manufacturers refused to sell them equipment because they didn't want their brand associated with mediocrity.

Then Sir David Brailsford stepped in with one simple philosophy.

Find 1% improvements *everywhere.*

They redesigned bike seats. Cleaned tires with alcohol for better grip. Adjusted hand-washing, massage gel, and even the pillows athletes traveled with.

None of it was flashy.

All of it was tiny and boring.

But together, those micro-gains compounded.

In 2008, the team that once went unnoticed won 70% of the gold medals in Beijing.

It works the same in life.

One clearer email. One cleaner system. One micro-fix in how people collaborate.

Suddenly, communication gets faster, meetings shrink, and problems get solved before they explode.

Big wins come from tiny, boring improvements. And science backs that up.

Researchers looked at thousands of workday journals and found something surprising. The number one thing that boosts human motivation is not praise, not passion, and not even purpose.

It's progress.

Even the smallest step forward creates a psychological lift.

When people made a tiny improvement, their creativity jumped, their confidence rose, and their momentum accelerated. Your brain doesn't need a massive achievement to feel alive. It just needs evidence that you're moving.

It reminds me of a story I heard when I was a kid.

ONE PEBBLE AT A TIME

In the old fable, a very thirsty crow finds a jug. It has water at the bottom but he can't reach it. Most animals would give up and keep searching, but not the crow.

He picks up one tiny pebble with his beak and drops it in the jug. Nothing happens.

Then he does it again. Still nothing. But he keeps going.

Piece by piece. Pebble after pebble. The water slowly rises high enough for him to get a drink. Through small, consistent effort, he reached his goal.

The crow didn't need a miracle. He just needed a place to start.

So, picture this. I call it The Ladder of Small Steps.

There's ridiculous power in *one*.

One step. One tenth. One choice. One minute. One win.

When you shrink something down to the smallest possible move, it suddenly becomes doable. Because even writing one sentence of the report, asking one clarifying question, or putting one plate in the dishwasher is enough to lower overwhelm and break the procrastination loop.

Research shows that even one tiny step can flip your whole mood and jump-start your motivation. And that's exactly what this image represents.

The ladder on the right demands giant, impossible leaps and is filled with excuses.

"It's too hard."
"I don't even know where to begin."
"I don't have time."

No wonder most people never leave the ground.

The ladder on the left is built from small, reachable rungs filled with ownership, effort, and patience.

"I can do one thing today."
"It matters enough to me that I'll make time for it."
"I'll ask for help."

Progress begins with the smallest action. Just start climbing. One simple step at a time.

One minute of focus. One small non-negotiable you follow through on. One honest conversation.

START SMALLER THAN YOU THINK

Living with **NO EXCUSES** is simple. It's about doing the little things that matter to you. It's taking ownership in the smallest areas of your life, 1% at a time.

So, what might 1% better look like to you?

Sometimes it just means noticing the world around you on your walk to the mailbox instead of racing through life on autopilot.

Being 1% better might mean putting away the contents of that box you just carried in from the car instead of leaving it in the corner of your living room for "later."

Or take 60 seconds to do The Daily 3 before bed tonight and review what's ahead so you can intentionally improve one thing tomorrow.

Just get it done. Stop excusing yourself. These tiny, boring actions are where self-respect is built.

One minute. One move. 1% at a time.

High performers don't look for breakthroughs. They master the basics. This is how elite teams create an edge that never looks impressive up close.

HIDDEN ONE PERCENTERS

THE ONE-DEGREE DIFFERENCE

Navy SEALs are legendary for impossible missions and unreal discipline. But here's the part most people miss. Their success isn't built on heroics. It's built on tiny, boring, microscopic corrections repeated so many times they become instinct.

In his memoir, SEAL Team Six, sniper Howard Wasdin talks about mission planning that required run after run of drills to catch tiny gear misalignments, half-inch padding issues, and one-degree compass errors.

One degree off doesn't feel like much in the moment. But a mile later, you're lost. That's not just a metaphor.

When SEAL teams swim underwater at night, they may experience total darkness except for the faint illumination of their navigation board. If their compass drifts even a single degree, they'll surface hundreds of yards away from their target. One tiny error becomes a complete mission failure.

So, what do they do?

They adjust. Constantly.

One degree left.
Half an inch down.
A breath slowed.

These adjustments look insignificant to the outside world, but inside the Teams, they're everything. Because SEALs know the truth.

You don't rise to the level of your goals.
You fall to the level of your habits

So, they constantly check the batteries in night-vision goggles. Straighten rifle slings. Secure clips.

A former SEAL summed it up perfectly.

"It's never the big things that get you killed. It's the tiny things you ignored."

SEALs survive because they notice what everyone else overlooks. Invisible to the world but life-or-death inside the mission. That's the power of hidden one-percenters.

And this isn't just true in the military. It's true in business, too. In fact, you've seen it delivered to your doorstep.

THE 1-CLICK REVOLUTION

Jeff Bezos, the founder of Amazon, built a global empire by obsessing over microscopic frictions customers didn't even notice. One of their biggest revenue jumps didn't come from some massive innovation. It came from a tiny tweak.

They replaced "Buy Now" with "1-Click."

That one button stored your shipping, payment, and preferences. It eliminated the entire checkout process. One tap and you were done.

A tiny shift.
One minute saved.
And it generated hundreds of millions of dollars in additional sales.

And it didn't stop there. Amazon looked for 1% improvements everywhere.

They tightened warehouse walking paths by just a few feet to save minutes per worker per shift. They redesigned packaging by centimeters so more boxes could fit in every truck.

They even shaved milliseconds off page load times because a tiny delay can tank a sale.

These hidden one percenter compounded into dominance.

Small things aren't small. Especially when you repeat them.

TIME TO STOP DRIFTING

One night before I began digging into **NO EXCUSES**, I realized that "normal life" discipline is a whole different beast than Olympic discipline.

Competing on ice, face-first at 90 mph? Easy.

Getting myself to stop doom scrolling? Apparently impossible.

I was frustrated with myself. I wasn't failing in big ways. I was just drifting in tiny ones.

A snooze here. A skipped habit there. Staying complacent with life. 1% at a time. Nothing huge. But it definitely added up.

I didn't even see it coming. I just felt stuck and frustrated because of it. It was a shoelace moment in my life. And I realized once again how powerful 1% can be.

For better or for worse.

Let me show you what I mean.

THE 1% RESET

We all love talking about getting 1% better, but almost no one talks about the truth you and I already know.

Shoelaces lose medals.

Which means that 1% worse hits us just as fast. And it compounds even faster. So, before we do anything uplifting or empowering, I want you to feel the *other* direction. The one you and I slip into without even noticing.

You don't even have to stand up. Just follow me.

Ready?

LET'S GO 1% WORSE.

Start with your breath.

Take a *shallow* inhale... and hold it for a few seconds.
Feel your body tighten, just slightly.

Now slouch. Just a little.
Let your chest sink and your shoulders slide forward an inch.
That tiny collapse signals your system to contract.

Add a small clench in your jaw.
Not a death grip. Just enough that your brain reads it as a warning.
Hold it there.

Now bring to mind something you've been avoiding.
The overdue task. The unfinished conversation. That stack of papers on your desk.
Notice how your breath shortens and your focus narrows.

Finally, lean your body just one inch off center.
Feel it. A tiny shift that instantly throws your balance off, even if no one else can see it.

There it is.

5 micro-moves. And your entire state drifted downward. Do you feel that?

No crisis.
No drama.

Just tiny choices quietly pulling you off your path. That's how fast 1% worse happens. One small, almost invisible shift at a time.

BUT HERE'S THE GOOD NEWS.

If 1% worse can change your whole state this quickly, 1% better can change it just as fast.

So, let's climb up. Let's go the other direction.

Instead of steps or lists, you get a single cue word.

RISE.

Every time you read the word RISE, you're going to make one tiny upward adjustment.

Start by resetting your body and breath.

Inhale slowly and then exhale. Feel your nervous system settle as your breath evens out.

LET'S GO 1% BETTER.

RISE: Place both feet firmly on the floor.
Feel the ground support you. Feel the steadiness underneath you.

RISE: Relax the muscles in your face. Your eyes, your jaw, your mouth.
Notice how your whole body softens the moment your face releases.

RISE: Lift your spine and roll your shoulders back an inch.
Not a posture makeover. Just a small adjustment. Feel your chest open and your energy rise with it.

RISE: Picture a place where your mind automatically softens.
Maybe it's your favorite chair, a quiet trail, or a time when you felt completely at ease. Let your attention expand instead of tighten.

RISE: Inhale slowly. Pause. Then let the breath go.
Feel your whole system come back into alignment.

Let yourself feel where you are now compared to a minute ago.

Subtle, right?

More grounded. More awake. More capable.

Tiny adjustments shape your mind and body. They make your day easier. Your health improves and you feel more capable of accomplishing the tasks in front of you.

1% worse pulls you down fast. 1% better helps you rise to your tasks.

So now that you've experienced this, what will you choose to do with it?

EXCELLENCE LIVES IN THE SMALL STUFF

DON'T TELL ME. SHOW ME.

In 2012, after having our second baby and then going through a late miscarriage, I did what every retired athlete swears they'll never do. I picked up the phone and told the new head coach, *"I'm coming back."*

As a World Champion and Olympian, I expected an enthusiastic welcome and maybe even a quick high 5 through the phone.

Instead, I got this.

"Noelle, I don't care where you've been or what you've done. All I care about is where we're going as a team. What you did in the past is in the past. So, I guess we'll see what you can do at the selection races this fall. Good luck."

Click. That was it.

I remember standing there thinking, *"Oh crap. Is this even possible?"*

MASTER THE MILLIMETERS

When you're a mom with 2 young kids and chasing an Olympic dream, you don't get luxury. You get margins. You get scraps of time. And you learn how to work every inch of them.

I didn't have endless hours to train anymore. So, I had to hunt for the tiny things that would actually move the needle.

And here's the part no one expects.

I cut my physical training from 6 days a week down to 3. I know it sounds backwards. But it was better. Much better.

Those 3 days were laser-focused and brutal in the best way.

Every rep.
Every set.

Every angle.
Nothing wasted.

NO EXCUSES.

My body thrived with the recovery between sessions. I was stronger, faster, and mentally sharper because I wasn't grinding myself into the ground anymore.

Outside of the gym, countless hours were spent lying on my sled on my living room floor and visualizing every track in the world. A stopwatch would help me gauge my timing and where I needed to make adjustments in my mind.

Skeleton is a sport of risks, anticipation, and micro-adjustments. You have to be prepared to move a split second before you're ready, or else you'll miss the whole thing.

I forced myself to feel the pressure, the fear, and the unpredictability of every curve. I anticipated the fans yelling and flashing cameras. I obsessed over eye movement, breath, timing, and shoulder drops measured in millimeters. I studied film, rewound mistakes, fixed them, and rewound again until my eyes refused to focus.

And it wasn't just the physical. I tightened up my mind too.

Music.
Movies.
Conversations.

If it brought me down, it was out.

And then there was my husband, Janson. My seriously amazing husband. He built me a new sled and used tech no one had ever seen before.

He upgraded the frame. Customized a saddle to fit my body like a glove. Designed the sled for aerodynamics and comfort. And he built a quick-release mechanism for my runners that reduced vibration. This innovation saved me precious minutes adjusting my runners between sliding runs.

Tiny changes everywhere.
Microscopic advantages.
But together, they added up.

When I focused on 1% improvements, everything shifted.

I sprinted faster.
I slid cleaner.
And I came back stronger than I'd ever been in my life.

REPEAT THE RIGHT THINGS

Looking back at my 2010 Olympic race, I didn't lose that medal because I wasn't strong enough, fast enough, brave enough, or committed enough. I lost it because I didn't have a system to catch the tiny things that mattered.

I relied on motivation instead of purpose. I relied on grit instead of structure.

And here is the truth most people don't want to hear. Your life doesn't change because of what you intend to do. It changes because of what you repeatedly do. When you repeat the tiny things, sustainable growth occurs.

Every transformation, whether it's in athletics, leadership, entrepreneurship, parenting, or health, comes down to one boring and very simple thing.

Notice one way to get 1% better.

Then do it.

FIX THE PART THAT'S FAILING YOU

When I realized that my shoelaces cost me a medal, I finally understood that the elite truly focus on the smallest details.

So, when I returned to the 2014 Olympics in Sochi, Russia, we made one-percent corrections everywhere we could find them and locked them into habits.

And yes... I got zippers on my spikes and covered those exposed shoelaces.

When all these small, boring, seemingly insignificant improvements were stacked together, my career changed.

I won more World Cup medals in those 2 seasons than I had in my previous 13 years of competitions.

Those shoelaces taught me that what you ignore today becomes what you regret tomorrow.

The little things you do or don't do will either cost you everything or carry you exactly where you want to go.

Your choice.

TALENT IS OVERRATED

Whenever my kids need a reminder of how excellence really works, I point them to one book.

Talent Is Overrated by Geoff Colvin.

Colvin studied world-class musicians, athletes, and leaders and discovered something surprising. The best wasn't the most talented. They're just intentional.

They improve in tiny, targeted ways called deliberate practice. Not glamorous. Not exciting. Just small, measurable corrections repeated over and over again.

Sound familiar? That's 1% better.

Colvin's research backs up everything I'm teaching you here. You don't win because you're naturally talented. You win because you're willing to make microscopic improvements long after most people get bored and quit.

THE 1% LIFE

At the start of this chapter, I told you the truth. Becoming an Olympian, or exceptional at *anything*, is VERY simple.

Be 1% better today.

That's it.

Not perfect. Not superhuman. Just intentional.

And when you live this way, your entire performance shifts. Results get sharper. Decisions get faster. You become the person people trust to get things done.

One little shift at a time, your life starts to feel different. And once you feel that momentum, you see the truth. Greatness never comes from giant leaps. It comes from the courage to keep showing up.

One small move at a time.
Every day.
Starting now.

CHAPTER 11

Lead in the Hallway

*"You give people power when you believe in them
before they believe in themselves."*
—Ed Mylett

THIS IS YOUR MOMENT

When you make the Olympic Team, you don't go straight to the Games. Team USA gathers every athlete in one place first. In 2014, that place was Munich, Germany. It was the last stop before racing in Russia.

While we were there, we learned from athlete ambassadors about what to expect at the Olympics. How to represent our country with class. And what it meant to wear USA across our chest.

And it's where we went through something mandatory and iconic called team processing.

All right, imagine this.

A massive empty warehouse the size of Costco, filled with row after row of Team USA gear.

Jackets. Shirts. Pants. Gloves. Goggles. Beanies. Bags. Opening and closing ceremony outfits.

You literally push a shopping cart through it all, trying things on, loading it up, and feeling like a kid in the most patriotic version of a candy store.

There's truly nothing else like it.

Once my shopping cart was maxed out, I took all the new gear back to my hotel room and started organizing it for our flight to Russia the next day.

I had to leave some things in the hallway because traveling with 2 young kids meant our room was already overflowing.

It looked like a minivan after a long road trip. You have everything you need. It's just covering every surface.

Toys here. Clothes there. And snacks in every corner.

In the middle of packing, I reached for a bag outside my door. As I did, I noticed my coach, Tuffy Latour, at the far end of the hallway. He was walking my way.

When he saw me step out of my room, he yelled my name.

"Noelle! I've got something for you."

Tuffy was a Sergeant in the National Guard, and everything about him reflected it. He carried discipline, integrity, and a calm strength you felt before he even spoke.

When he reached my room, he pulled his backpack off his shoulder and opened it up. Then he reached in and pulled out a silver jacket.

I knew exactly what it was.
It was the podium jacket.
The one only the medalists would wear.

Tuffy lifted it in his hands carefully and unzipped it.

On the inside, printed across the back lining of the jacket, something was written. He held it open so I could read what it said.

There were 4 words.

"This is your moment."

He looked me in the eyes and said with full confidence, *"Noelle, this is **your** moment."*

Tears filled both of our eyes.

He knew what it had taken for me to get there. He knew what Janson had sacrificed. And he knew what my kids had endured.

He knew the steep road we'd all climbed together.

In that quiet, ordinary hotel hallway in Munich, Tuffy gave me more than a jacket. He gave me something every great leader gives the people they serve.

He gave me belief.
He gave me his time.
And he gave me the confidence to show up as the strongest version of myself when it mattered most.

THIS IS YOUR MOMENT AS A LEADER

Hallway moments happen every day, but many leaders miss them because they're not looking.

But here's the real truth.

This is *your* moment.

Not someday when life finally slows down. *Right now.* In the middle of the meetings, deadlines, Slack pings, and constant change.

This is your moment. As a leader, a mentor, a coworker, a husband, a wife, or a friend.

Leadership is built in the moments when you don't want to slow down. But you choose to anyway.

So why is it that we miss them?

Let's pull back the curtain for a second because your brain is actually trying to do something else.

TEACH YOUR BRAIN TO SHOW UP

Your brain has one job.
Keep you alive.

Which means it's always scanning, jumping, and getting pulled into 5 things at once. It's a survival mechanism. That's why it's so natural to get distracted.

But practicing being present flips that switch.

It activates the part of your brain that handles clarity, focus, and emotional regulation.

When you show up, you show others that you believe what they have to say is important. And belief is powerful.

WHO BELIEVED IN YOU?

Stop for 60 seconds and answer this.

Who believed in you before you believed in yourself?
Really think about it.

Somebody did. Someone pushed you forward when you were scared to move.

Maybe it was the boss who said, *"You're ready,"* even though you felt like a fraud.

Maybe it was the teacher, the parent, the spouse, or the friend who pushed you past your own limitations.

Their confidence lifted you. It changed your trajectory. And it shaped who you became.

Who stepped in when you needed it most?
What did they see in you that you didn't yet see in yourself?

Belief can change a life. And sometimes, it even saves a life.
Let me tell you about the belief that brought home Apollo 13.

BELIEF IS CONTAGIOUS

APOLLO 13

I grew up hearing space shuttle stories from my Grandpa Wright. He worked on the Apollo missions during the 1960s.

He was the guy checking heat tiles, making sure every piece was up to standard so astronauts could survive the brutal re-entry back to Earth. One mission he spoke of with reverence was Apollo 13.

Apollo 13 launched on April 11, 1970.

During a routine tank stir 2 days later, a damaged thermostat overheated the wires inside an oxygen tank. It ignited and the spacecraft exploded. The astronauts were 200,000 miles away from the Earth.

In that moment, Gene Kranz, NASA's flight director, didn't panic and he didn't point fingers. Instead, he stood in the middle of mission control with a calm, grounded presence and one unshakable belief.

My team can solve this.

That belief spread like oxygen and immediately focused the minds on the problem that needed to be solved. And that belief brought 3 astronauts home alive.

Belief is contagious. But unfortunately, so is its absence.

THE COST OF BEING ABSENT

Your team always knows when you're not really there. They feel the disconnect instantly. And most of the time, it isn't because you don't care. It's because you're buried under excuses that sound like urgency.

Too busy. Too tired. Too much on your plate.

But those excuses cost you hallway moments. And hallway moments are where culture is built.

You've worked with leaders like that.

Leaders who are too distracted to notice your effort and too overwhelmed to see your potential.

When excuses run the show, effort drops and initiative dies.

So, here's your checkpoint.

The Zoom camera's off again.
Do you check in or do you ignore it?

A message pings while someone is talking with you.
Do you immediately respond to the text or finish the conversation in front of you?

Burnout is written across someone's face.
Do you pause or push?

These moments feel like interruptions but they're not. This is the space where real leadership lives.

BELIEF DRIVES PERFORMANCE

Here's what the research actually shows.

When people trust their leader and feel supported, they aren't just a little more engaged. They're nearly 3X's more engaged. That's huge.

Google proved this too. In Project Aristotle, the number one predictor of a high-performing team isn't talent or experience. It's psychological safety. It's the belief that your leader has your back.

That's what belief does. It lifts people up and inspires them to be more than they thought possible.

THE TICKET WITH MY NAME ON IT

As a rookie, I dreamed of making the World Cup team but I couldn't get out of my own way. I kept trying to feel confident, but all I felt was doubt and fear.

One afternoon, during our summer national team camp in Calgary, Canada, I didn't feel ready. But I was chosen. And that changed everything.

We had just finished a strength workout in the gym when one of my coaches, Greg Sand, quietly pulled me aside. He glanced around with an almost sneaky smile that said, *"Pay attention."*

Then, he reached into his pocket and pulled out a plane ticket.

It wasn't just any ticket. It was a ticket to the first World Cup race of the season.

He pointed to the top and locked eyes with me to make sure I saw it. It was my name. Printed in bold letters.

I stared at it, confused, because tryouts for the World Cup team were in 2 months. He explained that for logistics, the coaches had to submit the names of the athletes they believed would make the team. The names could be changed if the results were different. But the truth was right in front of me.

The coaches expected me to be one of them.

My heart skipped and a smile spread across my face.
He nodded and simply said, *"I believe in you, kid."*

He pushed the ticket back into his pocket and walked away.

It felt like a door opened that I hadn't known was locked.
The potential was always there. But his belief unlocked it.

That's what real leadership does. It hands you a version of yourself you haven't met yet. It shows you what's possible before you can even see it.

That conversation in the corner of the gym only lasted a minute or 2. But it changed me. I carried the belief of my coach into tryouts. Ready to step into who I was becoming and ready to race as one of the best athletes in the world.

You have opportunities to ignite this change in others as well.

Here's an easy tool you can use to unlock that same confidence in your team in less than a minute. It's called Hallway Leadership.

HALLWAY LEADERSHIP

Hallway Leadership is almost never about a hallway. It's about the moment between moments. It's the parking lot walk, the elevator ride, and the one-minute pause before a meeting starts.

So, here's what you do in those in-between spaces.

Notice someone.
Say their name.
Then, look them in the eye and call out one strength you genuinely believe.

"I see how hard you're working."
"Your ideas have been sharp lately."
"You handled that project with real maturity."

These tiny acknowledgments change people. They tell someone they're appreciated and seen.

You want a better team? Give them 60 seconds of presence.

That is Hallway Leadership.

CALM UNDER PRESSURE

TURNING SETBACKS INTO SOLUTIONS

5 years before the 2014 Olympics, my sled was in transit to the World Championships and was broken beyond repair.

Completely unusable.

This meant I had to borrow a sled. And let me tell you something. Skeleton sleds are *not* shareable. They are custom-built to your body, your weight distribution, and your steering quirks.

Taking someone else's sled down a 90-mile-an-hour ice chute isn't bravery. It's a death trap. And my results reflected it.

I was frustrated. My coaches were frustrated. And Janson was beyond frustrated.

But as setbacks often do, that moment lit the spark.

It made Janson determine that having to borrow equipment wasn't just inconvenient. It was unsafe and unacceptable. And he was going to change it.

Janson has a background in technology management and 3D design, which means his brain solves problems most people never even notice. So, right when we came home from that race, he turned to me and said something only a true problem solver would say.

"I'm going to build you a sled."

I laughed out loud. Hard. Random people don't build Olympic sleds.

When I realized he was serious, all I could say was, *"You get to take it down the track first."*

He spent the entire summer studying the spec book page by page. Learning every rule and every detail required to refine and build a legal skeleton sled.

And he did it.
He actually did it.

That is what **NO EXCUSES** looks like.

It was an incredible design, and I raced on it at the 2010 Olympics.

WHEN REGULATION DISRUPTS INNOVATION

When I came out of retirement in 2012, Janson made it his mission to build a sled that was faster, smoother, and sharper than anything I had ever raced on before. He tore through the entire spec book again. He studied every update and rebuilt every millimeter of the sled with intention.

1% better here. 1% better there.

When the season arrived, we traveled to Calgary, Canada, with our 2 toddlers for the first international race of the season.

My sled was measured, weighed, and evaluated. It passed inspection. It received the stamp of approval and it was ready to race.

But the next day, everything changed.

Overnight, the international rulebook shifted. We didn't even think that was possible, but it happened anyway. And out of every sled in the world, the new regulation would disqualify only one sled.

Mine.
The one Janson built.

You know this feeling. You build something brilliant. You innovate. You solve a problem no one else could solve. And then a policy, an update, or a regulation drops out of the sky, and everything you created suddenly becomes noncompliant.

Welcome to tech. Welcome to leadership. Welcome to the world we live in, where innovation moves faster than the rules that try to govern it.

I would have been disqualified without warning, but a friend on the jury told us the truth. Officials had rewritten the rules because of something impressive Janson had created.

One day it was legal. The next day it wasn't.

Janson could have exploded. He could have blamed the officials or thrown the sled into the corner and walked away. But he didn't.

He stayed calm. He stayed focused. And he went straight into innovation mode.

That's leadership in real time.

A few hours after finding out about the rule change, we pulled our rental van into a Wendy's parking lot to grab fast food for our family of 4.

And that's when the excuses began to flood my mind.

Doubt. Worry. Exhaustion. Frustration.

But before I could open the restaurant door, Janson stopped me. He saw the despair written all over my face.

He put his hands on my shoulders and said,

"Hey. Don't go there. You wanna know why? The rule change means other nations are scared. They see what you're doing. They know you're coming back strong. And they're afraid you're going to beat them. And you know what? You're going to prove them right."

That's leadership too. A hallway moment on the sidewalk outside of Wendy's.

His confidence calmed me. It helped to pull me out of panic mode and back into preparation for the big race ahead. He drew sketches of sled parts and asked for help. He rebuilt what needed to be rebuilt so we could get back on the ice.

Disruption hits. Regulations shift. Deadlines tighten. People panic.

Great leaders stay in the present. They respond instead of react. And they believe in their teams.

Janson's calm became my calm. And that sled went on to win multiple international medals. Including an Olympic one.

THE TEAM MIRRORS YOU

Researchers at Harvard and the University of Michigan found something remarkable.

A leader's emotional state is contagious.

When a leader stays calm, problem-solving improves. Working memory strengthens. And stress levels drop.

When a leader spirals, the team mirrors it within minutes.

Yale's research goes even further. They proved that stress spreads before you even say a word. People feel your tension the second you walk in.

When you regulate yourself, your breath, your tone, and your presence, you regulate the entire room.

PROCESS ORIENTED, RESULTS DRIVEN

That season and the next were full of sled disruptions, rule changes, and protests against my equipment. There were moments when I completely lost it. And moments I didn't think I could take one more setback or disruption.

But every time the frustration hit, Janson kept me from spiraling further. And my head coach, Tuffy Latour, stepped in with the same steady outlook.

"Don't worry about it Noelle. We'll figure it out. Let's just focus on being process oriented and results driven."

That was such a powerful statement. One that reminded me to keep placing one foot in front of the other. 1% here. And 1% there.

So, I'm going to repeat it.

Focus on being process-oriented and results-driven.

That motto pulled my mind out of the chaos of podiums and medals and back to the small details that actually moved me forward. It taught me to adapt quickly, pivot without panic, and clear the noise in my head.

And over time, that motto taught me how to focus on what mattered most, do the little things and anchor myself in the present moment

BE WHERE YOU ARE

Look at the image.

The adult is holding a child's hand, but their mind is somewhere else. You can see it in the cloud above their head.

Money. Work. Emails. To-dos. Deadlines. Worries. Noise.

They're standing in a beautiful field, but they can't see any of it.

Does this resonate with you?

The child, on the other hand, is fully there.

Their mind is clear.
Their attention is on the wildflowers right in front of them.
They see what's around them.

There's only one letter difference between the two.

Mind full versus mindful.

This is what presence feels like. You are either living the moment you are in, or you are living inside the noise in your head.

THE ANCIENT PRACTICE BEHIND PRESENCE

For more than 2,500 years, Zen Buddhist and Taoist monks trained their students to enter each moment on purpose. Their instruction was simple and powerful.

Pause at the doorway.

They believed every threshold was a gate. And before crossing it, students passed through 3 inner gates.

They used this imagery to train the mind to reset quickly, let go of the moment before it, and arrive fully in the one that was coming next.

Even ancient philosophers described something similar.

Marcus Aurelius wrote about entering the present moment as if stepping through a portal and leaving behind whatever came before it.

Different cultures. Same principle. And the lesson is this.

Wherever you are, be there.

Presence isn't accidental. It's trained.

And in the fast-paced, constantly changing, distraction-filled world we live in, leaders need this more than ever. Because you can't show up for what's next if you're still stuck in what just happened.

So, let's walk through the 3 inner gates together to feel our awareness expand and practice being fully present.

Gate 1: Breathe.
Gate 2: Notice.
Gate 3: Choose.

Here we go.

THE 3 GATES

GATE 1: Just Breathe.

Sit tall. Let your shoulders drop. Let your hands rest.

Now take a slow breath in through your nose.

Feel your belly rise as the air fills you.

And then exhale for longer than you inhaled. Let it fall out of you like a slow release.

Feel your body soften as the breath leaves.

Do it again.

A slow inhale.

A longer exhale.

Let your nervous system settle. Let your breath bring you into the moment.

GATE 2: Notice what's around you.

Now let your breath return to a natural rhythm.

Feel the contact of your body with the chair or the floor.

Feel the weight of yourself being held.

Notice the air on your skin.
Notice the temperature of the room.

Let your attention widen.

Hear the closest sound.

Then hear the farthest one.

Sense the space around you without needing to change anything.

Let the moment come into focus without effort.

This is what the monks trained. A mind that stops racing ahead or dragging behind.

A mind that returns to the moment you're actually in.

You're here now.

GATE 3: Choose how you'll show up.

Now softly ask yourself this.

Who do I choose to be in this moment?

Calm.
Present.
Focused.
Listening.
Grounded.

Let the word you choose settle into your breath.

Let it fill your body with intention.

Let it shape how you enter whatever comes next.

Take one more slow breath.

Feel the inhale.

Let it out. Feel the longer exhale.

Do you feel that?

You didn't rush into this moment. You entered it with intention.

MAKE IT PART OF YOUR DAY

You just disciplined your mind. You brought yourself back into the moment on purpose.

This is why ancient teachers practiced the gates. They knew the mind needs a transition. A moment to reset. A chance to choose.

Neuroscience confirms what they understood long before we had the language for it.

Presence is a skill.
It takes practice.
And it doesn't take much time.

You can pass through the **3 Gates** in less than 60 seconds.

You can do it in the hallway, in the car, before a meeting, or right before a difficult conversation.

Gate 1: Breathe.
Bring your body back into the moment.

Gate 2: Notice.
Open your awareness to the room or place you're in. Let yourself actually be here.

Gate 3: Choose.
Decide who you want to be as you step into what comes next.

This is how you become fully present.

WHEN LEADERS LISTEN

WHAT REED HASTINGS TAUGHT ME ABOUT PRESENCE

I once shared the stage with Reed Hastings, the co-founder and longtime CEO of Netflix. Backstage, he was calm, thoughtful, and fully present. He made you feel like you were the only person in the room.

Reed believes the hardest part of leadership isn't getting people to listen to you. The hardest part is getting them to tell you the truth.

At Netflix, honesty isn't just encouraged. It's expected. They understand that innovation doesn't come from silence. It comes from people who feel safe enough to speak up. And it comes from leaders who actively listen.

So, here's your question.

If someone on your team had feedback that could change your next decision, *would they tell you?*

WHY BEING HEARD CHANGES EVERYTHING

According to research from the Workforce Institute at UKG, 74% of employees say they're more effective at their job when they feel heard at work.

Think about that.

Not when they get a raise. Not when they get a new title. People come alive when they feel heard.

When leaders slow down enough to actually listen in the hallway, in the email, or in the meeting, everything changes.

Results climb.
Teams connect.
And culture strengthens from the inside out.

Being heard changes how people feel.
Being believed in changes how people show up.

LEAD WITH BELIEF

Now imagine how your entire workplace would speak up, take risks, and stop holding back if you led with one simple mantra.

"I believe in you."

Not occasionally, but consistently.

Imagine saying it to the engineer who just broke a build and looks terrified to tell you.

"I believe in you."

Imagine saying it to the analyst presenting for the first time and second-guessing every slide.

"I believe in you."

Or to your team after a failed sprint review.

"I believe in you."

When leaders respond with belief instead of blame, people open up and communicate more effectively.

They take ownership.
They move with confidence.
And they step up.

Try it for 7 days.

Lead every tough moment, every mistake, every stretch project, and every pressure-filled meeting with "I *believe in you.*"

Watch what happens. You'll see your culture start to reflect the belief you model every day. John Wooden is a great example of this.

THE LEADERSHIP LESSON WOODEN LIVED

John Wooden wasn't just an incredible coach. He was a master at teaching presence. After ten national championships, one of his most powerful lessons was this.

Be quick, but never hurry.

Quick means you see the moment right as it happens. It means being intentional and aware of your surroundings. Hurry is distracted and sloppy. Hurry is the birthplace of excuses.

Excuses like *"I'm too busy," "Not right now,"* and *"I'll check in later."*

Hallway Leadership asks you to be quick to notice the people and moments around you. Quick to take 60 seconds to breathe, reset, and choose your presence.

Never hurry past the people who need you most.

THIS IS YOUR MOMENT

Before the 2014 Olympics, in a quiet hallway in a German hotel, my coach looked me in the eyes and said, *"This is your moment."*

Those words reminded me of everything that had led me to that point. And they reminded me why I was there.

I walked into the Olympics with an ownership that I hadn't felt before. I knew that this was my moment to show the world what I was capable of. And it was a moment I wanted to share with all those that had made the dream possible.

Wherever you are right now, this is *your* moment.

You don't have to be perfect. You don't have to have all the answers. You only have to be present.

Presence creates connection.
Connection creates trust.
Trust removes excuses and lifts you and your team.

So, the next time you find yourself in a hallway, between meetings, between goals, or between seasons, remember this.

This is *your* moment.

CHAPTER 12

Live Your Legacy

"We live our legacy every day, not when life is over."
—Jay Shetty

THIS IS THE MOMENT

Every loss, challenge, and effort came down to this single moment.

One run. One minute. One last chance to finish the story I'd been writing for half my life.

Millions were watching, but that wasn't the pressure I felt. The real weight was knowing this was it.

My final race.

I'd competed a thousand times before, but the energy at the 2014 Olympic Winter Games in Sochi, Russia, was different for me. Everything seemed to move in slow motion. The athletes. The crowd. Even the falling snow seemed to freeze in place, like the universe was giving me a chance to take it all in.

And in that stillness, I didn't feel fear or stress or the need to perform.

Instead, I felt gratitude. A deep, steady, and pure gratitude for every setback, every comeback, and every person who carried me to this start line.

I had raced down the track 3 times and this chapter of my life was about to close.

I climbed into the shuttle with my sled and sat down. It was taking me to the top of the track for my fourth and final run of my career.

Suddenly the whole journey started playing in my mind like a highlight reel on double speed.

I saw my 16-year-old self.

Mom took time off work to drive me an hour each way to Park City. Through icy snowstorms, windy canyon roads, and rush hour traffic. I was convinced that if I just kept showing up, maybe, just maybe, this crazy sport might take me somewhere.

There was the sting of missing out on high school dances, parties, and friends because the skeleton season didn't care about Saturday nights.

College.
19 credits.
Division 1 track.
Training until my legs shook so hard I couldn't stand straight. Exhaustion was my major.

And my parents.

The sacrifices they never talked about. The money they stretched. The moments they set aside so I could chase a dream none of us fully understood.

I also thought about my husband, Janson.

The sacrifices he never advertised. The nights he tucked handwritten notes into my suitcase because he knew the homesickness would hit before the competition ever did.

Every memory had a weight. And every bit of that weight carried me straight into this moment.

The shuttle pulled up to the top of the track and we dragged our sleds out into the cold.

The driver gestured with the standard script. *"Be safe. Watch your step."*

He didn't want any accidents on his shift.

I nodded, but honestly? I wanted to say, *Buddy, I've bled for this.*

The cuts.
The bruises.

The E.R. visits.
That was Thursday for me.

My college teammates used to look at the black and green bruises on my legs like I needed an intervention plan.

Here's what they never understood.

Those battle marks meant I was still in the fight for the dream that mattered.

I set my sled down in Parc Ferme while jury officials stared at every inch of every sled like they were hunting for cracks in someone's character.

And instantly my mind went back to one of my own tests.

A Latvian hotel lobby.
Burlap carpet.
The night before a World Cup competition.
And a kinesiology final backed by a promise I wasn't willing to break.

I'd given my professor my word. I wouldn't open my books during the test.

I knew I'd be studying deep into the night while the rest of the team slept. But before they headed to bed, a teammate glanced at my book and smirked.

"Just cheat so you can get some sleep. Seriously, who's gonna know?"

I sat in disbelief.
I would know. And that truth hit harder than fatigue ever could.

So, at 2 A.M., I took that exam without shortcuts. **NO EXCUSES.** I kept my word.

I went to bed exhausted. And proud.

Honestly, taking a final in that old Latvian lobby with sticky, stained burlap carpet should've counted as extra credit. But it all worked out.

I won the World Cup gold a few hours later.

But the medal wasn't the greatest victory. The real victory was choosing integrity when the stakes were high.

Integrity is the decision you carry with you. It shows up in every arena of your life. Whether anyone sees it or not.

I left Parc Ferme and walked into the start house to get warm.

The room was packed, and the tension hit the second you walked in. I moved to my corner, sat on the wooden bench, closed my eyes, and let Enya drown out the noise.

A wave of memories rushed in again.
All of them.

The highs.
The heartbreaks.
The moments that shaped me and the ones that nearly broke me.

The bobsled that shattered my leg.

Becoming a World Champion.

Janson building my sleds.

When my 2 kids, Lacee and Traycen, were born.

Finishing fourth in 2010.
I retired to be home. But the miscarriage of our third child and Janson's quiet determination brought me back.

And as quickly as the memories hit, they faded, and the reality of the moment snapped into focus.

My playlist was now playing *"The Good Stuff"* by Kenny Chesney. I stepped outside to start my warm-up.

I looked around the venue and thought about my family waiting in the cold at the bottom of the track. My parents and siblings in the stands. Hearts pounding harder than mine. Everyone had sacrificed to get me here.

Janson, Lacee, Traycen, and I had lived in hotels for 2 years chasing this dream.

My eyes teared up as I thought about all those that loved and supported me on this journey. I looked at my watch, wiped my eyes, and flipped the switch in my brain to the task ahead.

It was time.

I was ready to make this moment count.
And just like that, the memories disappeared.

The lights blurred.
The crowd vanished.
And the noise shut off like someone hit the stop button on Spotify.

All I could see was the track in my mind.
The lines. The angles. The exact path I needed to take.

I was ready.
Ready to take on this run and carry with me every person and every
moment that brought me here.

I slipped into my speedsuit, tightened the strap on my helmet, and walked
out to the start.

My coach, Tuffy, was waiting for me. He looked way more nervous than I
felt, and I wanted to break the tension. I wanted to see him smile.

"This is awesome," I said, grinning. *"This is the Olympics."*

He laughed, shook his head, and muttered, *"Get after it."*
I knew he wouldn't be able to relax until I crossed the finish line.

The green light flashed.

The next 60 seconds would rewrite the next chapter of my life.

This was it.

I sprinted. Loaded onto my sled. And the world disappeared.

I honestly don't remember anything about the run. It was a blur. On a day
when everything seemed to move in slow motion, the 60 seconds of racing
on the ice was over in a blink of an eye.

I definitely stepped into "the zone." The space where there's no fear and
no hesitation. It's a place where nothing can distract or derail your focus.
Everything just... clicks.

It was crazy. Like I pushed off of the starting block and immediately finished.

Nothing in between.

When I crossed the finish line and climbed the long hill toward the scoreboard, everything came back into focus.

"How did I do? Where did I finish?"

One of my coaches rushed out and threw his hands in the air. And that was the moment I knew.

My best had been enough.

That run sealed an Olympic medal.

The second my sled stopped, I jumped off my sled and practically tackled him with a hug. Every emotion I'd ever tucked away came rushing to the surface at once.

Immediately, the Olympic volunteers motioned for me to celebrate my minute of fame with the countless camera crews in the media zone. But all I wanted in that moment was to get to my family. They were only a few yards away, but it felt like miles.

I frantically looked for a way to reach the ones I loved, but with the crowds of people packed in and staircases blocked, I could only see one logical way to get to them.

Go up and over.

Adrenaline rushed through my body.

I leaped over the icy track wall.

Jumped up and grabbed the steel bar of the bleachers.

And then somehow, I managed to pull myself up and over the railing to embrace my family.

I found my kids. My parents. My siblings.

As I reached for Janson, the moment said it all.

"We did it! We did it!"

Because this moment wasn't mine alone.

It was ours.

I had fulfilled my purpose for being there. I had defined success on my own terms. And ultimately, I had stepped straight into the legacy that moment would become.

LIVE THE STORY YOU WANT REMEMBERED

LEGACY LIVES IN THE LITTLE THINGS

Legacy isn't built in grand gestures. It's built in the tiny, intentional things you do on ordinary days.

The words. The kindness. The integrity.

One small comment can become the spark that rewrites a life.

When teenage Steven Spielberg screened a rough little 8mm film, a teacher pulled him aside and said, *"You have a gift, Steven. Don't stop."*

That's what leaving a legacy looks like.

It was a hallway moment. And he never forgot it. It nudged him toward the life he was meant for.

Every decision, big or small, creates a moment that matters. You may never realize which moment becomes someone else's turning point or which small interaction becomes the one they remember most about you.

So, keep showing up. Keep choosing the small things that make a real difference for others.

HOW LEGACY CHANGES YOU

Loyola researchers found that when you define your legacy, it flips a switch.

Your confidence rises. Your identity tightens. You begin acting like the person you want to become instead of the person you used to be.

And here's the surprising part.

Legacy thinking also lowers regret. Because when you're clear on the life you want to leave behind, you naturally ask yourself where your decisions will lead you.

Consider this for a second.

If today was on repeat, would it take you where you want to go?

If the answer stings, that's your invitation to change.

THE LIFE YOU'LL WANT TO REMEMBER

When your story ends, what do you hope people say about you?

Zoom out with me for a minute.

Imagine you're 99 years old, sitting somewhere peaceful, looking back on your life. You feel proud. You loved people well. You kept growing. You used your time on things that mattered. And you don't have many regrets.

From that perspective, ask yourself this.

What mattered most to me?
Who was I, really?
How were other people's lives better because I was here?

Whether you realize it or not, that's your legacy.

Now let's dive in a little deeper.

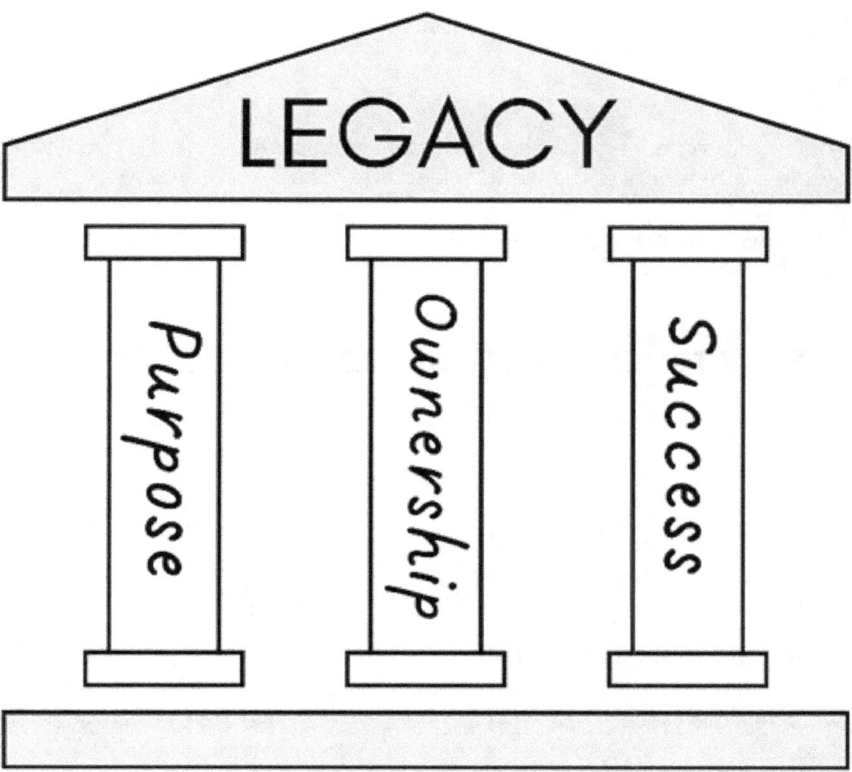

Creating the legacy you want rests on the 3 Pillars of Legacy.

First is purpose.

This is your long-term purpose. The one rooted in your values.

Purpose shows you what matters and what doesn't. When you know your purpose, you can tell the difference between a real limitation and an excuse.

Second is ownership.

This is accountability in action. If you don't take ownership for your life, then excuses will write your story. And when that happens, you'll never stay aligned with the purpose you claim to care about.

Third is success.

Not anyone else's version of success.
This is your definition.
Your terms.

You've got to define success for yourself and update it often. If you don't define it intentionally, the world will do it for you.

When these 3 Pillars of Legacy lock in, they leave a lasting imprint of who you choose to be.

THE STATEMENT THAT SHAPES YOUR STORY

Let's look at the first pillar.

Purpose.

You can't live aligned if you don't know who you are.

So, ask yourself the one question most people avoid:

What is the purpose of my life?

Don't tell me you're *"still figuring it out."* Purpose isn't something you determine someday. Purpose is something you determine today.

So, let's get personal.

It's time to create a purpose statement. But before you write yours, I want to share mine. This is the statement I return to when I need clarity. It helps me align my choices and call out my excuses, day after day.

"The purpose of my life is to be a disciple of Jesus Christ and cherish my loved ones, to pursue lifelong learning and growth, and to strengthen and share my gifts so that I might inspire others to live more fully, love more openly, and make a greater difference today."

This is my compass. My filter. My boundary.

It reminds me what I want my life to stand for and what I refuse to let excuses steal from me.

So, now it's your turn.

CREATE YOUR PURPOSE IN 3 SIMPLE STEPS

Step 1: "The purpose of my life is to..."

If it will matter to you when you're 99, then that's a great place to begin.

Maybe it's living aligned with your faith or building a strong and loving home. Maybe it's leading with courage instead of fear.

Ask yourself:

What matters most to me?
What will always matter, no matter the season?

Here are a few ideas to get you started.

- Be generous with my time and resources

- Create things that bring hope, clarity, or beauty into the world

- Guide others with honesty, humility, and strength

If your mind goes blank right now, don't panic. Mine did too the first time. I sat there thinking, *"The purpose of my life is to... make it through the day?"*

But we can definitely do better than that.

Start with whatever rises to the surface. It doesn't need to be perfect. It just needs to be honest. You can always refine it later.

Step 2: "To..."

This is who you're becoming.

What talents do you want to strengthen?
What skill, habit, or quality do you want to develop?

Maybe it's patience, presence, or leadership. Maybe it's sharpening your communication or deepening your spiritual life.

Try these on.

- Strengthen my talents through practice and dedication

- Use my influence to lift others

- Release judgment and love openly

Step 3: "So that..."

This is the impact piece. It's the reason your purpose matters.

How do you want someone's life to be different because you were in it?
Do you want people to feel inspired, encouraged, seen, or supported?

Here are a few directions you could go.

My work brings clarity, beauty, or light into someone's life

People believe change is possible for them

People around me experience more joy, gratitude, and peace

YOUR PURPOSE - THE 3 STEP TEMPLATE

Now put it all together:

The purpose of my life is to ________________________________,

to ____,

so that ____.

That's your purpose statement. One clear, honest framework. And it's *yours.*

Here are 2 more examples in case you need them.

Example 1

The purpose of my life is to live with integrity and lead by example.

> **To** keep learning and using my voice to lift others **so that** people feel empowered to grow and do what they once thought they could not do.

Example 2

> **The purpose of my life is to** turn my struggles into strengths. **To** keep healing, growing, and sharing my story with courage **so that** others believe change is possible and find the strength to keep going.

Your first draft might look messy. Good. Mine did too. Purpose statements are like selfies. You take 20 before you get that you're willing to show anyone.

But when you do this, your decisions will sharpen, your integrity will steady and you'll shut down your excuses.

Purpose is the pillar of your legacy. It wipes out comparison and judgment because you stop measuring your life against anyone else's. And when you live from that clarity, you start building a legacy your 99-year-old self will look back on and say, *"Yes. That's who I chose to become."*

THE S.I.X.T.Y. SECOND SHIFT™

Excuses never show up in loud or dramatic ways. They show up quietly.

"We should postpone until we have perfect information."
"The team isn't ready yet."
"We need more data before we decide."

And here's the part most people don't realize.

You don't talk yourself *out* of excuses. You talk yourself *into* them.

Every excuse you've ever surrendered simply began as a moment you didn't interrupt.

The argument. Procrastination. The overscheduled calendar.

So, if you want to stop excuses from running your life, you need a way to interrupt them. Fast. Before your brain hands the wheel to fear, habit, or comfort.

That's where the **S.I.X.T.Y. Second Shift**™ comes in.

It gives you a 60-second window to shift out of the excuse and into action.

If you don't shift, excuses will always steal away what matters most to you.

Time. Faith. Opportunity. Identity. Relationships.

And it's not just personal.

This shows up in boardrooms. Zoom calls Sprint planning meetings. And every tough conversation you'd rather postpone.

Excuses go first everywhere.

WHERE EXCUSES ACTUALLY WIN

Let me show you what this looks like in real life.

Have you ever had a moment where you know exactly what you *should* do, and then you do the opposite on purpose?

That was me and the remote. My brain was like, "Let's grow," and my hand was like, "No."

The struggle is real.

Part of my own purpose is *"to pursue lifelong learning and growth."* But night after night, without thinking, I'd reach for the remote.

Doing it every now and then might not make a big difference in life. But 5 months of a poor habit? Or 5 years? That will absolutely drift you away from the purpose you say you want to live.

That's why I created the **S.I.X.T.Y. Second Shift**™.

Neuroscience shows that you only need a few seconds to interrupt an excuse and take back control.

The moment one of the 5 Excusers show up, you've got 60 seconds to act before they take the lead.

So now, when I reach for the remote, I notice that it's the justifier. And it's excusing its way into my night.

This is the exact moment the **S.I.X.T.Y. Second Shift**™ process begins.

THE S.I.X.T.Y. SECOND SHIFT™: HOW TO BEAT YOUR EXCUSES

S - See it different

Excuses trap you when you accept them without question. Seeing it different means recognizing that an excuse is not the truth. It's a thought trying to keep you comfortable.

Remember, you can't change what you refuse to see.

I - Imagine tomorrow

Then picture tomorrow. Picture yourself. Picture the thing you're avoiding.

See it unfinished.
Still waiting.
Still nagging.
Still weighing on you because you walked past it again.

Now flip it.

See the project finished. A chapter read. The wall finally painted. The email sent.

How do you feel?

As Simon Sinek says,

"The person you hope to become is shaped by the choices you make right now."

When you imagine tomorrow, today becomes simple.

X - Xpect resistance

Resistance isn't a sign that something is wrong. It's a sign that something *matters.*

Your brain will feed you every excuse it can find to keep you comfortable. That's what it's wired to do.

Expect it. And move anyway.

T - Take one step

Not ten. Not the whole project. Just one step.

Put down the remote. Open the book. Lace the shoes. Clear the desk.

Excuses can't survive movement.

Y - You decide who you are

Every time you choose action over excuse, even a small action, you cast a vote for the person you're becoming.

The life you've always wanted to live is only S.I.X.T.Y. seconds away. Don't put it off any longer. When you take 60 seconds to choose your actions, you are choosing to move toward the life your 99-year-old self will thank you for.

THE GYMNAST WHO FLIPPED THE SCRIPT

During a high-performance coaching session with the University of Utah gymnastics team, I watched something powerful happen.

This team competes for a national title every year. They know the stakes, and they know what excuses can cost them.

So, I asked them a simple question:
"What do you tell yourself in the exact moment doubt or fear hits your body?"

The room went quiet.
Then the team captain raised her hand.

She said,

"I've learned to see it differently. When I feel anxious, I tell myself it's not fear. It's excitement."

Then she continued.

"So, instead of saying that I "have" to be here, I tell myself I "get" to be here, and then I act like it. And that changes everything for me."

I just stood there smiling because she had mapped out the **S.I.X.T.Y. Second Shift**™. Every step of it. Without ever hearing the framework.

She lived it. And once the rest of the team heard her, teaching the process became effortless.

S.I.X.T.Y. SECONDS. THAT'S ALL IT TAKES.

Successful leaders, elite athletes, and high-performing individuals follow the same pattern. Spot the excuse, then do the **S.I.X.T.Y. Second Shift**™.

See it differently.
Imagine tomorrow.
Xpect resistance.
Take the step.
You decide who you are.

This pattern works with any goal. Any struggle. Any season.

Use it, and you take back control. Repeat it, and you build the ownership that defines a **NO EXCUSES** life.

LIVE THE LIFE YOU WANT TO LIVE

MOMENT OF THE GAMES

I didn't understand the impact of that moment in the stands following my Olympic race until we flew home from the Games.

But then the letters arrived.
From people I'd never met.

Parents who showed up with more intention. Couples who reconnected. Families who remembered that winning means nothing if you can't share it with the people who matter most.

That jump into the stands didn't belong to me anymore. It belonged to everyone who saw themselves in it.

At the Team USA gala a few months later, the prestigious "Moment of The Games" award would be given to the individual or team who demonstrated the pinnacle moment that represented what the Olympic spirit and Team USA are all about. Nominees were presented by the United States Olympic & Paralympic Committee and then voted on by the country.

When my name was called to the stage, I was stunned. The moment that the people chose to celebrate wasn't a gold medal, a record-breaking time, or a massive score. It was the celebration of gratitude and love.

My legacy wasn't the medal. My legacy was the embrace.

DEFINE SUCCESS FOR YOURSELF

I'm so grateful I took the time to define success for myself long before the results were posted. In the months leading into the Olympics, I pictured what success would truly mean to me.

It wasn't a medal. And it wasn't recognition. It was giving my best and doing it with my family. If I did that, I couldn't fail.

If I had allowed the world to define success for me, it would have been based on the color of a medal. And I would have believed that I had failed.

What a loss that would have been.

A silver medal, imperfect on paper, was perfect to me only because I had already chosen my own definition of success. And that choice became contagious to the millions who watched.

Success isn't complicated. It's alignment. It's doing what matters most instead of doing everything. Success is about doing the right things. The things that align with your purpose.

So, here's your 60-second challenge for today: Define success for *this* week.

Your health.
Your relationships.
Your work.

What matters most right now?

Finish the sentence: **"This week will be a success if I..."**

Really think about this.

Define success each week, and it becomes the third pillar that your legacy is built upon.

Purpose. Ownership. Success.

LIVE A LEGACY YOU'LL BE PROUD OF

Legacy isn't built in decades. It's built daily. In small, quiet, ordinary moments that stack into a life you are proud to live.

The next 60 seconds hold more power than you think.

So, take a breath and look at the moment in front of you.

This is where your legacy is made.

It grows every time you choose purpose over distraction, action over excuses, and alignment over drift. It grows when you notice yourself slipping and choose to steer back. It grows the moment you decide, *"This is who I choose to be."*

Your legacy won't be defined by perfect days. It will be defined by the intentional ones.

It will be defined by the days you show up in the hallway moments that matter to someone else.

That is the legacy you build in the next 60 seconds. And that is a legacy worth leaving.

LIVE A LIFE WITH NO EXCUSES.

This book wasn't written to inspire you for a moment. It was written to equip you for a lifetime.

And here's what matters most.

Real transformation begins with simplicity.

60 seconds of courage.
One intentional choice.
Over and over again.

You now know how to shut down excuses when they show up and choose ownership instead.

And that ownership will transform your life, your team, and your results.

The toughest person you will ever lead is yourself.

So, live with mercy in the middle.
Choose progress over perfection.
Use the next 60 seconds well.

Then repeat.

Because when you choose who you want to be in the next 60 seconds, you shape the kind of person you'll become today, next year, and throughout your life.

So, here's my simple invitation to you.

Live the next 60 seconds with NO EXCUSES.

Acknowledgements

To my family, thank you for your patience, your belief, and the countless quiet sacrifices you made while I chased an idea that mattered deeply to me. You carried more so I could focus more, and I'm truly grateful for it.

To the coaches, mentors, teammates, leaders, and friends who challenged me, pushed me, and refused to let me settle. Thank you for teaching me that growth is earned in small, often uncomfortable moments. Your lessons live in these pages.

To the professionals who helped shape this book, sharpen its message, and bring clarity to the chaos of early drafts, thank you for your skill, honesty, and commitment to excellence.

And to every person whose story, insight, or example influenced these ideas. Even if your name doesn't appear here, know that your impact does.

Finally, to you, the reader. Thank you for choosing ownership. Thank you for being willing to look honestly at your choices and take responsibility for what comes next.

This book isn't about perfection.

It's about progress.

And progress is never a solo effort.

About The Author

Noelle Pikus Pace is an Olympic silver medalist, World Champion, keynote speaker, corporate coach, and leadership advisor known for helping leaders drive results and make better decisions under pressure.

After stepping away from elite competition to focus on family, Noelle made a daring return to skeleton, the world's most dangerous winter sport. Racing headfirst down an icy track at highway speeds demanded discipline, clarity under pressure, and the willingness to act even when fear and excuses were present. Her determination earned her an Olympic silver medal and shaped the leadership philosophy that defines her work today.

Noelle's clients include Fortune 100 companies such as Amazon, Walmart, AT&T, and Procter & Gamble, as well as leading firms like Deloitte and Accenture. She enables leaders and teams to align priorities, take decisive action, and drive performance. Her work extends to shaping a culture and mindset where teams feel empowered, supported, and ready to take action.

"I've learned that progress is built in the next decision, the next action, and often the next 60 seconds."—Noelle

No Excuses brings these principles to life through stories from the Olympic track, leadership research, and everyday moments where choices quietly shape outcomes. At its core, the book is about recognizing that progress is built in the next decision, the next conversation, and often the next 60 seconds.

Noelle lives in Utah with her family, where she continues to speak, coach, and teach leaders how to move forward when standing still would be easier.

BRING NOELLE TO YOUR AUDIENCE!

Olympic Mindset. Executive Execution. No Excuses.

Noelle Pikus Pace is an Olympic silver medalist, 2x World Champion, and globally sought-after performance strategist who helps organizations eliminate excuses, accelerate decision-making, and execute under pressure.

For more than a decade, Noelle has partnered with Fortune 500 companies, high-growth organizations, and elite teams to build cultures of ownership where clarity replaces hesitation, accountability replaces burnout, and results follow consistently.

She doesn't motivate people to feel better.

She teaches them how to perform better.

WHY NOELLE WORKS FOR EXECUTIVE & CORPORATE AUDIENCES

Today's leaders don't need more inspiration.

They need faster decisions, stronger ownership, and teams who execute without waiting.

Noelle brings the same skill set that carried her to the Olympic podium, under injury, loss, pressure, and imperfect conditions, and translates it directly into business, leadership, and team performance.

Her work helps organizations:
- Cut through overthinking and stalled momentum
- Increase speed, clarity, and follow-through
- Build emotionally disciplined leaders
- Replace excuse-driven cultures with ownership-driven results

THE NO EXCUSES PERFORMANCE METHOD

At the core of Noelle's work is a deceptively simple principle:
Sixty seconds of ownership can change everything.

In high-pressure environments, excuses don't show up as weakness.
They show up as:

- Delayed decisions
- Over-analysis
- Perfectionism
- Comfort-driven leadership
- Missed opportunities

Noelle teaches leaders and teams how to identify excuses in real time and shut them down before they cost momentum, morale, or results.

And because sustainable performance requires humanity, not harshness, her framework places "Mercy in the Middle" at the center of every decision, ensuring accountability without burnout.

KEYNOTE & PROGRAM OUTCOMES

Audiences leave Noelle's sessions able to:

- Make clearer decisions faster, even under uncertainty
- Execute without waiting for confidence or perfect conditions
- Build emotional discipline instead of relying on motivation
- Lead themselves first, increasing credibility and influence
- Create consistent results across teams and departments

This is practical, repeatable performance not hype.

WHO SHE SERVES

Noelle has delivered keynotes and leadership programs in 8 countries across 4 continents, working with organizations including:

AT&T • Deloitte • Amazon • Walmart • Comcast • Kellogg's • Liberty Mutual • Lucid • Vivint • Qualtrics • ESL Faceit Group • Pluralsight • LearnUpon • InsideSales and more.

Her message resonates with:

- Executive teams
- Sales organizations
- Leadership development programs
- High-performance and growth-focused cultures

CREDENTIALS THAT COMMAND THE ROOM

1. Olympic Silver Medalist
2. 2x World Champion | World Cup Champion
3. 26x World Cup Medalist
4. First American Female World Champion in Skeleton
5. United States Olympic Committee "Moment of the Games"
6. TEDx Speaker – The Color of a Medal
7. Utah Sports Hall of Fame | UVU Hall of Fame
8. Honorary Doctorate, Utah Valley University.

IDEAL FOR

- Leadership conferences
- Sales kickoffs
- Executive retreats
- Organizational change initiatives
- High-performance team development

THE RESULT

Organizations don't leave inspired.

They leave aligned, decisive, and executing.

Because the toughest person you will ever lead is yourself and that's where performance begins.

BOOKING & INQUIRIES

www.noellepikuspace.com

Keynotes • Leadership Intensives • Executive Coaching